T0150345

RETURN TO YAKNI CHITTO:

HOUMA MIGRATIONS

PHOTOGRAPHS & ESSAYS BY MONIQUE VERDIN IN CONVERSATION WITH

T. Mayheart Dardar

Anesie and Jane Verdin

Allison Rodriguez

Raymond "Moose" Jackson

Kathy Randels

& Nick Slie

Edited by Rachel Breunlin

The Neighborhood Story Project
An imprint of
The University of New Orleans Press

All photographs by Monique Verdin
unless otherwise noted.

Excerpts of Raymond "Moose" Jackson's poems "ancestor poem" and "the fish story"
published with permission
from ArtSpot Productions and Mondo Bizarro's *Cry You One*.

Excerpts of the poem "in pointe-aux-chenes" and *The Loup Garou: A Lunar Cycle*
published with permission from Raymond "Moose" Jackson.
Special thanks to Lavender Ink.

Cover image:
Melinda, Melena, and Beau Verdin in Grand Bois, 2000.

Series Editor: Helen A. Regis
Graphic Designer: Gareth Breunlin
Photo Editor: Bruce Sunpie Barnes

The Neighborhood Story Project
P.O. Box 19742
New Orleans, LA 70179
www.neighborhoodstoryproject.org

This project was made possible with generous support from
the Surdna Foundation's Thriving Cultures Program,
the Office of Academic Affairs at the University of New Orleans,
and the Boebel Family Foundation.

Traditional Architecture | **Bayou Pointe-aux-Chenes** | **Early 20th Century**

This photograph was taken in front of my great-grandmother Celestine's cypress home that was built with a mud and moss chimney and palmetto roof. Celestine is pictured in the front row second from the far left, and my other great-grandmother, Ernestine, is on the far right. Also pictured here is *traiteur* Nonc Oban (*third from right in first row*), a traditional healer in the Pointe-aux-Chenes community, and my grandmother's best friend, Jean Verdin (*the young woman seated, fourth from the left, in front row*). Photograph courtesy of the Verdin family.

Skeleton Oak | **Pointe-aux-Chenes** | **2005**

Inside the Yakni Chitto, the roots of live oaks singed by salt waters have left gray silhouettes—reminders of the groves that once thrived along the bayou banks of the old Pointe-aux-Chenes ridge. When I photograph them, I think of how someone once told me the spirits of the ancestors dwell inside old skeleton trees.

DEDICATION

To Rosalie Courteaux
&
the granddaughters
of the Yakni Chitto.

And to the memory of
Armantine Billiot Verdin
Jeanne Verdin
Marcelite Naquin
Herbert Verdin
Xavier Verdin
Lawrence "Pete" Billiot
Robert Billiot
Marcellin Roussell
&
Buster Naquin

Armantine and Savin Billiot | **Bayou Pointe-aux-Chenes** | **Late 1910s**
Portrait of my grandmother and her brother by an unknown photographer, courtesy of the Verdin family.

ACKNOWLEDGMENTS

Without the life force of the Mississippi River delta, her sacred waters and unpredictable natural intelligence, these words and images, experiences and stories, would not exist. May we find new, and return to old, ways that honor and regenerate her dynamic system to heal past damages and to restore sustainable relationships for generations to come.

I am incredibly grateful to all the women in my life who have challenged me to face my greatest fears and who have inspired me to keep seeking out life's dreams, feeding my soul with love, laughter, kindness, compassion, wisdom and strength; especially my grandmother Armantine Marie Billiot Verdin and my momma, Renee Neyrey Mack, as well as Vivian Hotard, Jeanne Verdin, Marie "Beb" Verdin, Jane Verdin, Carol Verdin, Clarice Friloux, Emelda Cheramie, Sheila Wilkinson, Ashlee Stokes, Sharon Linezo Hong, Mercedes Rodgers Thomin, Heather MacFarlane, Allison Rodriguez, Ama Rogan, Cammie Hill Prewitt, Jayeesha Dutta, Kathy Randels, Brenda Dardar Robichaux, Janie Luster, Corrine Paulk, Tara Gass Braden, Rebecca Snedeker, Rebecca Solnit, Ashlee Wilson Michot, Robbin Boyd, Kaili Boyd, Ruth Verdin, Veronica Verdin, Tammy Greer, Rachel Reeves, Marie Françoise Crouch, Hannah Pepper Cunningham, Suzanne Dhaliwal, Pat Arnould, Yudith Nieto, Elizabeth Rappaport, Mollie Day, Valentine Dyson, Cindy Livingston, and the talented and patient editor of this book and so many other incredible Neighborhood Story Project publications, Rachel Breunlin.

Thankful for my fathers: My dad, Herbert Michele Verdin, and my stepfather, James Mack, whose unconditional love and years of hard offshore work out in the Gulf of Mexico provided for our unconventional family.

Mark Krasnoff's life left an unforgettable impression on mine. He continues to influence the way I look at the world every day, as well as the work I have put my heart into ever since.

Much appreciation for writer Roger Hahn for finding me my first apartment at 1510 Euterpe Street back in 1999, giving me my first warning that the Houma documentary project would be a lifetime of work, and encouraging me to enroll in my first college classes while still pursuing this lifework as a witness and artist.

Words cannot explain my gratitude for Alessandra Moctezuma and Mike Davis's facilitation in presenting and connecting our realities of South Louisiana to fellow Americans, providing a foundational experience and continued support, providing a catalyst for public engagement, and adding fuel to the fire to continue recording and analyzing the issues.

I've been blessed to have a most unconventional education in life with a spectrum of characters who have offered critical analyzes and personal philosophies, experience, and knowledge. Super grateful for all those I consider my teachers and, in some cases, have been lucky to call them collaborators as well: Houma historian T. Mayheart Dardar; keeper of the Bayou Bienvenu Triangle, John Taylor; and photo makers Barry Kaiser, Leslie Parr, Owen Murphy, Victoria Ryan, the infamous David Richmond, Seth Boonchai, David Rodrigue, E. Paul Julian, Jonathan Travesia, Alex Nunez, and Michel Varisco.

The heart of a good organization is grounded by the special people who make the magic happen. I have been so fortunate to have been a past artist-in-residence at Tulane University's A Studio in the Woods. The first time was a year and a half after Hurricane Katrina, and I had the opportunity to live with the founders, Lucianne and Joe Carmichael, during my Restoration Residency. I often say that the Carmichaels introduced me to some of my best friends, including Raymond "Moose" Jackson and many other past residents and friends of A Studio in the Woods. At almost 30, I developed a relationship with that bottomland hardwood forest on the banks of the Mississippi River, which shifted my perspective of the very place I call home. I am forever humbled and filled with so much gratitude.

Also connected to my beloved A Studio in the Woods creative family tree are ArtSpot Productions and Mondo Bizarro, two of the oldest and most avant-garde theater companies in New Orleans. Our work together has helped my personal storytelling practice to evolve and has helped to open up a whole different world of engagement with the delta that I never could have imagined without the experience of building *Cry You One* with them out on the levee bordering the central wetlands of St. Bernard Parish.

Other organizations and institutions that have been critical relationships supporting my work include St. Bernard Parish's Los Isleño Cultural Complex, the Meraux Foundation, Torres | Burns Trust, Crevasse 22, Loyola University New Orleans, Tulane University's New Orleans Center for the Gulf South, Los Angeles Social Public Art and Research Center, Centro de Arte La Regenta, San Diego's Mesa Community College, the Indigenous Environmental Network, the United Houma Nation, New Orleans Academy of Fine Art, and Another Gulf is Possible.

Special thanks to Trevor Schoonmaker for his curatorial invitation to participate in New Orleans' international art triennial Prospect 4, which provided the opportunity to reflect on the last 20 years of my documentary collection at The Historic New Orleans Collection.

Jane and Anesie Verdin have been my surrogate nuclear family down Bayou Pointe-aux-Chenes. More than family, they are my elders, teachers, and friends, who have provided the gateway for me to reconnect with my father's ancestral lands and waters. Without their generous love this work would not have been possible. Thank you to T. Mayheart Dardar, Raymond "Moose" Jackson, Jane and Anesie Verdin, and Allison Rodriguez, who have allowed their voices of witness to be woven into the lines of this book project. Thank you to Kathy Randels and Sean LaRocca for reading early drafts of the book, and to Kathy and Nick Slie for contributing writing to our final chapter. And to my family who have shared their lives, helping to inspire this record: Charles and Joanette, Beau and Brynan Verdin, T'Dun, Annette, Cody, Justin and Adam Verdin, Hannah and Taylor Naquin, Leonardo Rodriguez, Dillon Verdin, Melina Verdin, Melinda Verdin, Brent Verdin, Chris Verdin, and Ernie Verdin.

So much appreciation for so many family members and family friends, including Robert Billiot; Kenneth Verdin; Blaise and Isabella Pezold; Danny Friloux and family; Bebe, Bernice and Katelin Billiot; Deanna and Tony Credeur; Al and Joanna Plaisance; Briar Plaisance; Roland Billiot; R.J. Molinere; Dex Verdin, Mark and Bracken Kirk; Dallas Goldtooth; Powell Miller; Eliot Barron; Kirah Haubrich; Andy, Nikko, and Indie Hong; Sean Linezo; Michel Bechtoille; David Bartee; Nick Slie; Adam Tourek; Kelly Campbell; Wayne Hixson; Jon Boyd; Timothy Jordan; Charles Watkins; George Marks; Tony Adrian; Marie's Bar; and all the good people of Grand Bois and the Pensacola Paradise Bar and Grill. Special thanks to Shane Bartels for reminding me that life is a cyclical journey, and that when you get lucky, it leads you down foreign, yet familiar, roads where sunsets and company are always better.

Since Hurricana Katrina, sharing delta curiosities and questions with others as we endure waves of loss and the promises of restoration have led to a series of ongoing conversations with an informal Delta Collective that has brought together unexpected interdisciplinary collaborations and relationships. I am so thankful that I have had the opportunity to dialogue with architects Anthony Fontenot and Jakob Rosenzweig, starting with exhibiting maps of the Mississippi Delta in conversation with my photographs, and now dreaming about physically building adaptations that can sustainably address the challenging conditions of change.

Deep gratitude to Marie Barronnet, Joe Denmon, Melisa Cardona, Libby Nevinger, and Sabree Hill for both documenting special moments in time and allowing the inclusion of those moments within the pages of this book; as well as for Jakob Rosenzweig providing his cartographic skills.

Tree of Life | **Grand Bois, Louisiana** | **2000**
Bottom to top: Allison Rodriguez, Chris Verdin, Leonardo Rodriguez, and Dillon Verdin.

Thank you to Neighborhood Story Project's production team: Bruce "Sunpie" Barnes for editing the photographs, Gareth Breunlin for designing the book, Helen A. Regis, NSP series editor, for encouraging us to explore the connections between the Houma and sugarcane plantations in south Louisiana, Chelsey Shannon at the University of New Orleans Press for doing a close read of earlier drafts of the book, and Abram Himelstein and G.K. Darby for seeing it to press. A special thanks to Michel Varisco for curating the traveling exhibit, Gareth and Chromo Graphics for the design and production work, and D. Ryan Gray in the Department of Anthropology & Sociology at the University of New Orleans, and the Boebel Family Foundation for helping us bring it to life.

TABLE OF CONTENTS

Marsh Home | **Pointe-aux-Chenes** | **2000**

The last "camp" past the Cut-off Canal down Bayou Pointe-aux-Chenes. The tropical storms and hurricanes of 2003, 2005, 2008, and 2012 broke the wooden building, more and more, to pieces. Apache Oil and Louisiana Land and Energy now hold the land rights.

PART I

GLOBAL CLIMATE CHANGE:
A HOUMA PERSPECTIVE

by T. Mayheart Dardar

Leo on Bayouside | **Pointe-aux Chenes** | **1999**

The first time I met my cousin, Leonardo Rodriguez, was on the bayouside at Jane and Anesie Verdin's home. He was just two years old.

Centuries ago, the Greek philosopher and scientist Thales of Miletus theorized that all of creation was based on water. For Thales, all of life was nourished and replenished by the waters beneath, above, or around it. These days, modern science has long moved on from Thales' speculation, but if it were to be repeated here in south Louisiana, I have no doubt it would still resonate within our coastal communities.

In the swamps and marshlands of the Bayou State, water and the dynamic interaction between wet and dry form the foundation of the lives and lifeways of the peoples of the region. For the Houma and other indigenous peoples who have made our homes amidst dark streams and moss-covered cypress, it is that interaction between land and sea, salt water and fresh, ebb and flow, that has held and continues to hold the keys to our survival. Fish, mammals, amphibians, and reptiles alike all depend on the delicate balance of elemental forces that control our sub-tropical ecosystem.

In painting, the liminal zone is called *sfumato*. Leonardo da Vinci explored it in the hazy, ill-defined borders around his most famous portrait, the *Mona Lisa*. As much a philosophical principle as an artistic technique, it gives us a soft transition between colors and objects, as well as illustrating the frontier between wet and dry, stable and unstable.

Houma culture and lifeways were forged in this fluid domain. The brackish waters between salt and fresh gave us subsistence and provided the foundation of our economy. From the medicinal plants that healed us to the fish and crustaceans that fed us, the land and waters were life. The relationship between people and place cannot be overstated; Houma identity is contingent on the nature and content of this traditional territory.

For over a century, unchecked economic development has ravaged our homeland. Its most visible result is coastal erosion brought about by the channeling of freshwater sources to serve the needs of commerce and the excessive intrusion of salt water into our freshwater estuaries because of dredging by energy corporations. The Louisiana coast has lost over 2,000 acres since 1930. The number grows every day.

This same unchecked economic development has a global impact beyond our shores, significantly contributing to the causes of global climate change. The irony for us is that the fossil fuels harvested at great cost to our local environment continue to affect us directly as they are burned around the world, raising global temperatures and returning to us in the form of catastrophic weather patterns and rising seas. These rising waters have the potential to turn our traditional lands and lifeways into an Atlantian memory.

As with all Indigenous Peoples, our existence and identity is tied to the lands and waters that have given birth to us. As the avarice of capitalism continues to devour our world, we wonder with our brothers and sisters around the globe, what will be left to pass on to our descendants?

they said they would love the land
and put by from their stores to feed it
to pay back what the land had given

and their children would live
amongst the gamma grass and roseau cane
and they would call this place kin

they would spin
fine stories and songs of the old country
to keep the land company
these songs they would tie into the nets
and stretch them across the sky
and haul in a load of stars
to twinkle in the tide

so great was the bounty
so deep their gratitude and reverence

—from "the fish story"
by Raymond "Moose" Jackson

Allison Rodriguez | **Bayou Pointe-aux-Chenes** | **2003**

PART II
RETURN TO YAKNI CHITTO

Pointe-aux-Chenes | **Early 20th Century**
My great-grandmother Celestine Verdin with some of her children. To the left is an unidentified relative. The photograph is taken in front of a traditional Houma structure built out of palmetto. Photograph courtesy of the Verdin family.

Introduction

In 1915, my grandmother, Armantine Marie Billiot, was born in south Louisiana. Matine, as she was known, grew up on a bayou sometimes called *Pointe-aux-Chenes* (Point of the Oaks) or *Pointe-aux-Chiens* (Point of the Dogs). Located between the Atchafalaya and Mississippi Rivers, the bayou runs inside the Barataria-Terrebonne estuary where land loss is now being experienced at one of the fastest rates on the planet. I first learned of the original name of our territory, *Yakni Chitto* (Big Country), from Houma historian T. Mayheart Dardar, whose work has helped us begin to reclaim the history and language of our people. Matine never referred to her homeland this way. She called the region by its French name *Terrebonne* (Good Land), and her specific home *La Pointe*.

When I was a girl, Matine dug out an old shoebox from the cypress armoire she usually kept locked to show me the only five photographs she had from her childhood. We do not know who took them. When she showed them to me, the pictures of our family seemed foreign to life in the United States at the end of the 20th century. They helped translate all the things she couldn't put into words.

When I asked Matine questions about who we were, she told me we were Houma Indians. In the Muskogee language, Houma means "red." The name *Oklahoma* (Red Land) comes from the Muskogee as well. When the French arrived, they called indigenous people in Louisiana *les sauvages* (those who live closer to the wild). Other colonial names followed: American Indian, Native American, Indian, and *les indiens français* (the French Indians). Living closer to nature describes part of how I was raised, a way I continue to try to live. As I grew older, I learned more complicated stories of who we are.

After the Shatter Zone

In the late 1600s and early 1700s, the cultural landscape of indigenous nations in the South went through dramatic changes as chiefdoms collapsed from epidemics and slave raiding. Old World diseases such as smallpox spread across the region even before European settlers arrived. Weakened from the mass death, Indian nations were vulnerable to outside attacks. British slavers hired Chickasaw warriors, armed with guns, to raid communities in what is now Florida, Alabama, Mississippi, and Louisiana. In the attacks, young children and the elderly were often killed, and those able to walk the long trails to port towns such as Charleston were sold into slavery as far away as the Caribbean and South America, but also to plantation owners in South Carolina and Virginia. The French colonizers of Louisiana often bought slaves from these raids as well. Scholars say low estimates of the number of Indians enslaved range from 20,000 to 50,000 people; the devastating consequences have led them to call the era the "Mississippian Shatter Zone." Along the Gulf Coast, many tribes relocated to the area between Mobile Bay and New Orleans to escape the raids, and new groups of people were formed.

During the Spanish Empire's rule of Louisiana (1763–1802), colonial officials encouraged the migration of other

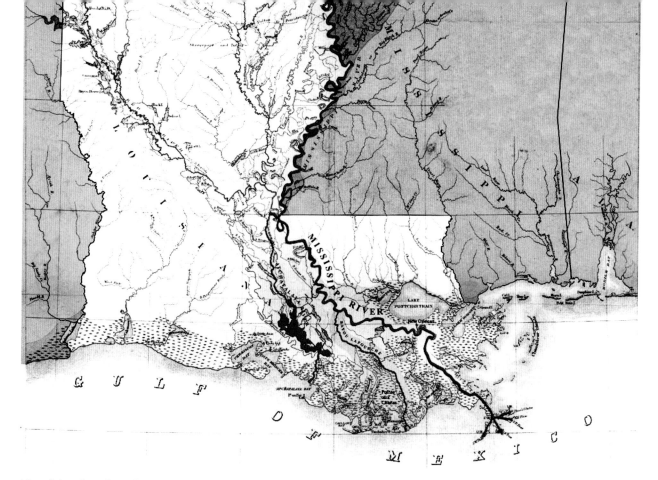

Map of the Yakni Chitto, by Jakob Rosenzweig.

groups into sparsely populated Louisiana to act as a buffer against the British. People as diverse as Acadian exiles from francophone Canada, Canary Islanders, and Filipino mariners found homes in South Louisiana, as well as Choctaw and Biloxi from what is now Mississippi.

Through oral history and genealogy, we know the modern Houma trace their ancestry back to the historic Houma who lived on the blufflands near where the Red River joins the Mississippi. They were pushed out by the Tunica and relocated near Bayou St. John in New Orleans, and back up to Ascension and St. James Parishes along the river. Through these relocations, they intermarried with other tribes in the region who were living in this era of empire: the Chitimatcha, Choctaw, Biloxi, Atakapa-Ishak, Acolapissa, Oucha, Chaouacha, Bayougoula, Tchoupitoulas

and perhaps other *petites nations* who survived the shatter zone but whose names have been forgotten and erased. While confederacies like the Cherokee and Choctaw held onto large tracts of tribal land and began to own African slaves themselves, our descendants interacted with the plantations through trade, but did not join in the business of slavery themselves.

The story of one of our ancestors, Touh-la-bay "Houma" Courteau, provides a glimpse into a world in flux. Listed as a "Biloxi Medal Chief" from the Gulf Coast, Touh-la-bay joined the migration west into Louisiana and settled along Bayou Terrebonne where he had a large family with an indigenous woman named Marianne who is thought to be from the cosmopolitan Mobile area. One of their daughters, Rosalie Courteau, was born in the late 1780s.

Rosalie's marriage to Jacques Baptiste Billiot created an important lineage amongst the Houma, and the Billiot name was passed down through Matine's family.

The ethnic identities of the Houma are complicated. Some lines of our family genealogy can be traced back to France. In other colonial documents, our relatives have been listed as "griffe." During the Spanish era, this designation was for mixed people of African and Indian ancestry. T. Mayheart Dardar explains why these parts of our history have not been readily acknowledged by our tribe:

> Years of suffering the effects of racial discrimina-
> tion had impacted the Houma to such an extent
> that they suppressed their own history. Any hint of
> African blood was denied for it was this fraction of
> African blood that had inspired their detractors to
> label them "Sabines," a racial slur.

This discrimination against multiethnic people has had real political consequences for the Houma. The United Houma Nation's petition for federal recognition was formally filed in 1985, and rejected by the Bureau of Indian Affairs in 1994. One of the main reasons they cited for denying recognition was the "mixed" status of the tribe. Although the tribe rebutted the decision in 1996, the B.I.A.'s recommendation to split into smaller groups to prove more direct bloodlines to indigenous heritage was accepted by some members of our tribe. The *Point-au-Chien* (Point of the Dog) Indian Tribe and the Biloxi-Chitimatcha-Choctaw Confederation of Muskogee bands (located along Bayou Lafourche, along Bayou Grand Caillou, and on Isle de Jean Charles) split from the United Houma Nation. The divide between coastal tribes is a scar in families that many are still healing from.

Unceded Territory

After the Louisiana Purchase transferred control of the area from the French to the United States, tribes in Louisiana did not sign treaties with the federal government. The Courteaus, Billiots, Verdins, and other families who were given Spanish land grants were able to hold onto their homeland

Jeanne Verdin with Family
Pointe-aux-Chenes Early 20th Century
Matine's best friend, Jeanne Verdin, sits at in the front row, second from right. Photograph courtesy of the Verdin family.

as individuals, but did not collectively bargain. As Louisiana changed from a territory to a state, Indian identities were erased in census records by American obsessions with race. With Indian people classified first as "people of color" and later as "black," tribal identities were not acknowledged. In the 1830s, the federal Indian Removal Act mandated that southeastern tribes east of the Mississippi River be removed to "Indian Country." New Orleans was a stop on the trails of tears. Without a political tribal identity, indigenous people in Louisiana were not forced to move. Nonetheless, the Removal Act emboldened settlers to take more land. When the Haitian Revolution collapsed the sugar industry in the French colony of Saint-Domingue, white settlers from all over the U.S. began sugarcane plantations farmed by slave labor in south Louisiana.

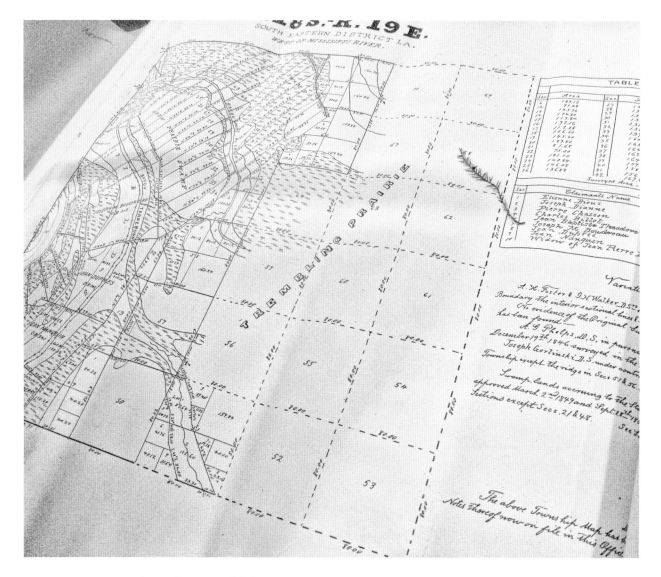

The Trembling Prairie | **Terrebonne Parish** | **1856**

Map "T.18S-R 19E," Southeastern District, La, West of Mississippi" shows Houma land, which extended to the "trembling prairie." According to Susan Brind Morrow in *Home Ground: Guide to the American Landscape*, "prairie is by nature trembling, being made of grass. The phrase seems to describe an interesting quality of optical illusion, that rising shimmer over a vast expanse of disparate entities, which, in the tumbling liquid motion of the wind, gives a panorama the appearance of a single living thing.... called *flotant* by the locals and often referred to as *la prairie tremblante*, a floating marsh not anchored to the ground beneath. It consists of tightly entangled plants and their roots, mixed with peat; typically, there is water flowing below it, over a layer of clay covered with oozing soil. In 1899, George W. Cable wrote in *Strong Hearts* of 'a maze of marsh islands—huddling along that narrow, half-drowned mainland of cypress swamp and trembling prairie, which follows the Mississippi out to sea.'"

Facing displacement, many Houma families began to move south to the ends of bayous Terrebonne, LaFourche, Du Large, Grand Calliou, Petite Calliou, and Pointe-aux-Chenes. They also lived out on Isle de Jean Charles and on Pointe Barré. In 1829, the city of Houma built their first courthouse where the Houmas last village once stood along Bayou Cane. When people tell me they had never made a connection between the tribe and the city, I am always shocked by the colonial amnesia—after kicking us off the high ground, they named "their" town after us and conveniently forgot we existed.

The wetlands, unwanted by plantation owners, became our refuge. In 1849, the U.S. Congress passed *An Act to Aid the State of Louisiana in Draining the Swamp Lands Therein*, which transfered federal land that had been part of the commons to the state. The goal was to generate income from the sale of land to develop drainage infrastructure and levees to protect sugar production. After the Civil War, Houma families sometimes worked as sharecroppers on these plantations during the harvest season, but then went back to making a living on the water.

Other families didn't have the same mobility. In 1887, 10,000 white and black sharecroppers from St. Mary to Lafourche Parishes went on strike for better wages. In retaliation, white militias attacked them. Black workers were forced off plantations, and an estimated 300 were wounded, killed, or went missing. In Thibodaux, reports of white paramilitaries killing people in the black community ranged from 35 to 50, with bodies found in shallow graves around the town. No one was ever charged.

Throughout the 20th century, justice in Terrebonne continued to be an ongoing struggle that was often thwarted by powerful men. U.S. Senator Allen J. Ellender was born on a sugarcane plantation in Montegut to an Acadian, French-speaking family. In his free time, he collected Indian artifacts. In Congress, he actively blocked civil rights legislation. In 1938, he filibustered a federal anti-lynching bill brought up after two black men, Roosevelt Townes and Robert McDaniels, were chained to trees, tortured with blowtorches, shot, and set on fire by a white mob in Duck Hill, Mississippi. Making his opposition to the bill clear,

Senator Ellender declared on the floor of Congress: "We shall at all costs preserve the white supremacy of America."

Back in Terrebonne Parish, the district court had created an at-large voting system that maintained this supremacy. Throughout the 20th century, organizing efforts by people of color to secure greater representation failed because they did not have individual voting districts. The issue of the 32nd District Court became extremely important around land disputes that developed when fur trappers, and then oil and gas companies, began moving into the area. My elders have told me stories of businessmen coming down the bayou to their isolated communities, promising financial benefits for "leasing" their lands. They were tricked into signing "X"s on contracts they could not read in exchange for 20 dollars and eviction notices. When they could not obtain a signature, companies turned to archaic laws that prevented "bastards" from inheriting property, as well as using unpaid taxes, to confiscate land.

Matine's Beginnings

My grandmother grew up on Terrebonne Parish's side of Bayou Pointe-aux-Chenes. Her best friend, Jeanne Verdin, lived on the east side claimed by Lafourche Parish. I never heard Jeanne speak anything but Houma French except for once. I perked up when I realized she had said "ice cream" in English. As young girls, Matine and Jeanne played in the prairie, rode calves, and trapped on their own. Imagine two little Houma girls carrying a big stick to knock out the animals caught in their traps. Matine told me once they were confronted by an older white man who told them to get off his land. They brandished the stick, yelling, "This is our land!"

I cheered, "You chased him away!"

Matine shook her head. "But we didn't keep him away."

When she was 18, she began a family with Jeanne's older brother, Toussaint Verdin. When I asked her about how they got together, she said, "He wouldn't leave me alone." She told me, "I know what love is, but I don't know what being in love is." She married him because she knew he was

Hoeing Sugarcane on Plantation | **South Louisiana** | **1930s**
Dorothea Lange's photograph of sugarcane workers in Louisiana taken for the federal government's Farm Security Administration. Houma joined black and white sharecroppers to work on the sugar plantations seasonally. Photograph courtesy of the Library of Congress.

going to be a hard worker. Their first son, Xavier, was born in August of 1934, but they didn't legally marry until the 1940s when they had their third child. Matine got her own birth certificate in the 1950s.

In the summer, they were shrimping, drying shrimp, and fishing for a living. They also sharecropped on sugarcane plantations like Hope Farm that was just above Pointe-aux-

Chenes. In the winter, they went to St. Bernard Parish, 60 miles away, to trap for large landowners near Bayou Terre-aux-Boeufs, once the corridor of some of the most wealthy sugarcane plantations in the region. They arrived right after the Isleños' struggle to hold onto the commons, which became known locally as "the Trappers' War."

Outside the Levee | **Bayou Terre-aux-Boeufs** | **2019**
Bayou Terre-aux-Boeufs, one of the most important distributaries of the Mississippi River south of New Orleans.

Bayou Road | **Bayou Terre-aux-Boeufs** | **2019**
In 1779, Canary Islanders, known locally as Isleños, began to settle along Bayou Terre-aux-Boeufs. Bayou Road was built by the Spanish colonial government as away for them to travel between their newly granted land and New Orleans.

A New Ride | **Pointe-aux-Chenes** | **Early 20th Century**
My grandfather, Toussaint Verdin, posing for the camera at the wheel of an old Model A Ford. Interestingly, when Ford first started making cars, they stuffed the seats with Spanish moss, which was also used in Houma architecture and mattresses because it is both water resistant and known to repel bacteria, mold, and insects. In this picture, you can see it hanging from the trees. Photograph courtesy of the Verdin family.

Trapper's Camp | **St. Bernard Parish** | **1941**
Working for the Farm Security Administration, Marion Post Wolcott photographed Isleño trappers outside of Delacroix Island in St. Bernard Parish. Photograph courtesy of the Library of Congress.

St. Bernard Parish

During Prohibition in the 1920s, liquor smuggling from Cuba and fur trapping in the wetlands fueled a roaring economy in St. Bernard Parish. The Isleño community, descendants of the Canary Island immigrants from the Spanish colonial era, had hunted mink, otter, and raccoons for more than a hundred years, but the national fur industry around the country began to call in a better price for muskrat as well. St. Bernard and Plaquemines Parishes became the most productive fur-producing area in the world.

Trappers' Boats | **St. Bernard Parish** | **1941**
Marion Post Wolcott's photographs of Isleño trappers outside of Delacroix Island in St. Bernard Parish include the homemade boats they used to navigate narrow waterways in the wetlands. Photograph courtesy of the Library of Congress.

Muskrat Run | **Marshes Near Delacroix Island** | **1941**
An Isleño trapper checking one of the traps he has set on a muskrat run. Image by Marion Post Wolcott, courtesy of the Library of Congress.

God Is My Judge | **Plaquemines Parish** | **1941**
Working as a Farm Security Administration photographer, John Vochon
captured signs along the side of the road in Plaquemines Parish, home
parish of Leander Perez. In this piece of public media, Perez is called
out for intimidation. Image courtesy of the Library of Congress.

The boom in profits led to land grabs. Formerly inde-
pendent trappers were now forced to pay land companies for the rights to the wetlands. Other landowners
began to hire trappers to undercut the Isleños. These
trappers, most of whom spoke Spanish, sought out the
political boss of Plaquemines Parish, Leander Perez,
who was also the district attorney of both Plaquemines
and St. Bernard Parishes. Under his leadership, they
established the St. Bernard Trappers' Association, but
soon learned he was purchasing large tracts of land

behind their backs. When they protested, he hired
gunmen to threaten them into submission. The trappers
held their ground, but Perez went on to use his position
to negotiate large profits from the oil and gas industry
that was being established in the same region. In the
1980s, for instance, it was discovered that he had been
paid 80 million dollars by oil companies through a secret
company called the Delta Development Corporation.

***Kenilworth Plantation* | Bayou Terre-aux-Beoufs | 2019**
Located at 2931 Bayou Road, in the late 1700s, Jean Chauveau purchased 30 tracts of land off Bayou Terre aux Boeufs from an Isleño who had been given land grants from the Spanish crown. Chauveau was from the French sugar colony Saint-Domingue. He built the house in a Caribbean, Creole vernacular, and lived here with a free woman of color named Constance Vivant. They mortgaged, and ultimately lost, the property. It was eventually sold to the Bienvenu family, who enslaved 13 people on the plantation. In 1887, it was bought by an Isleño, Albert Estopinal. A Confederate veteran who grew up in Toca Village in St. Bernard Parish, he spoke Spanish, French, Creole, and English.

In the aftermath of the Trappers' War, Houma began to come to St. Bernard Parish seasonally to trap. My grandparents went through the migration cycles for a couple of years, and then Matine told Toussaint, "Look, we're either going to stay here, or we're going home. But I'm not going back and forth anymore."

There was small band of Houma who were working together. Matine's cousin, Orlie Billiot, bought a piece of property on the land where the Kenilworth Plantation was located. My grandparents bought eight acres right next to him. The Dardars bought a piece of property right next to them. And then the Hotards. They all lined up by the

St. Bernard Catholic Cemetery, one of the oldest in Louisiana. My elder cousin Vivian Hotard asked me, "Why you think we're all on this side of Terre-aux-Boeufs bayou?"

I honestly didn't know: "Why? Because... *because?*"

"They wouldn't let us buy land on the other side of the bayou because the white people lived on that side!"

I was not aware of the legacy of slavery and segregation in St. Bernard. The Houma's recent migration connected us more to the bayous in Terrebonne and Lafourche than to what had happened up and down Bayou Road.

Clue to the St. Bernard Massacre
Bayou Terre-aux-Beoufs | 2019

When I first started taking photographs, the priest at the old St. Bernard Catholic Church asked me if I would document all the old tombs and headstones in the cemetery. Established in 1787, it is the fourth oldest Catholic cemetery in the Archdiocese of New Orleans. I was learning about "white balance" in my 35 mm black and white photography class, and the assignment was perfect for learning the skill. I remember being so confused the day I stumbled upon Pablo San Feliu's tombstone that read "Assassinated by Slaves, Incited by Carpetbag Rule," years after the Civil War had ended.

In the days leading up to the presidential election between Horatio Seymour, a Democrat, and Republican Ulysses S. Grant in 1868, 35 to 100 freedmen were killed by mobs of white men in St. Bernard Parish. Pablo San Felieu was killed in retaliation, and this gravestone was most likely put up some time afterward, which accounts for the incorrect date.

2824 Bayou Road | **Bayou Terre-aux-Boeufs** | **2000**
My grandfather, Toussaint Verdin, traded guide services to hunters for lumber in order to build this cypress home for his family in St. Bernard Parish.

Vivian was from Point Barré, a Houma settlement in Terrebonne Parish where oil was first discovered in 1929. The oil industry ran the community out of the area. She moved to Pointe-aux-Chenes before settling in St. Bernard Parish and finding work in a greenhouse.

In St. Bernard, people were discriminated against by color more than last name. In Terrebonne and Lafourche, surnames like Billiot, Verdin, Naquin, Dardar, Solet, Dion and others immediately identified people as "Indian." A Houma elder, Corinne Paulk, recalls segregation signs in the region reading: "Whites," "Colored," and "Indian." In St. Bernard, they were not immediately identified as one particular background. They blended in with the Isleños, Italians, Creoles and Filipinos. They were able to find work. Their kids were allowed to go to white, public schools. Toussaint started cutting grass for the Parish, and was one of Sidney Torres's head trappers. Matine couldn't read and she couldn't drive. She stayed home with their seven children. As a summertime hustle, she grew okra on their land, and Toussaint drove their truck over to the French Market in New Orleans to sell it.

Vivian's Pecans | **Bayou Terre-aux-Boeufs** | **2003**
When they weren't picking crab meat or making filé out of sassafras, Vivian and Matine spent their fall days together picking pecans to sell for a little extra money.

Lodi and Harris Dardar on Front Porch | **Bayou Terre-aux-Boeufs** | **2000**
Raised together in Pointe-aux-Chenes, Harris and Matine were first cousins, but my grandmother thought of him more like a brother. When her own brother, Armand "Lovency" Billiot, didn't return from World War II and Harris did, he married Armand's widow, Lodi. They migrated to St. Bernard Parish where they raised their family, and grew old together in Violet.

In the late 1950s, the Houma people who settled in St. Bernard organized around the right to vote, and they tried to get Toussaint involved. He wouldn't get on board with them. Vivian said some were mad at him for pulling back. I think he remained silent in fear of rocking the boat and losing the rights they had gained by moving to St. Bernard. Judge Leander Perez's staunch segregationist stances scared everyone.

During the 1960s, white families from the Lower Ninth Ward of New Orleans began moving to St. Bernard Parish during white flight from the desegregation of public schools in Orleans Parish. Perez dared civil rights activists to follow. On national television, he showed the dungeon-like concrete cells at Fort St. Philip in Plaquemines, built during the Spanish colonial era in 1792 and surrounded by barbed wire, and threatened to lock anyone up who challenged the existing order. Leander never used it, but he was excommunicated by Archbishop Joseph Francis Rummel for opposing the desegregation of Catholic schools. He also worked to prevent a deal with the federal government for Louisiana to share oil royalties from off-shore drilling because he was angry at Harry Truman for desegregating the armed forces. People of color in New Orleans still talk about being scared to visit Plaquemines and St. Bernard Parishes.

With Eyes Wide Open: Nonc Savin Billiot | **Poydras, St. Bernard Parish** | **2003**
My grandmother's brother, Savin, joined the Houma migration to St. Bernard Parish after
World War II. He was a really good mechanic who could make any lawnmower work. As he got
older, his eyelid refused to blink and would stay shut all the time. He remedied his ailment with
a piece of scotch tape or simply with his finger when he wasn't working on a machine.

Herbert Michele Verdin (1953–2006)
Bayou Terre-aux-Boeufs | 2004
My father loved to remind me: "People look, but they don't see. They hear, but they don't listen." He had a warrior's spirit. His gift of making people laugh was his medicine.

My dad, Herbert Michele Verdin, came of age in this era. He was the baby boy of the family—the favorite, the fun one. A down-the-road brown boy with long black hair. When he walked into the room, people would light up, happy to see him, ready for him to make them laugh. It wasn't enough to keep him out of danger. In the early 1970s, he was playing pool with a couple of friends in a barroom down in Plaquemines near English Turn. Two parish cops, not dressed in uniform, walked in. I'll never forget the look on his face when he told the story of what happened next. They beat him, cut his hair, and locked him in an old cell down on the east bank of Plaquemines at Pointe a la Hache, not too far from Fort St. Philip. When his sister arrived to bail him out, she didn't recognize him. He had to tell her, "Millie, it's me."

Around the same time, Matine's life got upended. Toussaint had a stroke. Their oldest son, Xavier, was hit by a car and suffered severe brain damage. In the mid-1970s, Toussaint went into the hospital again. He started feeling better and Matine said he even looked different—like he was well enough to get up and walk out of the hospital. He passed away hours later. Matine received his social security check. Combined with Xavier's disability, they were able to get by with a garden growing and a freezer stocked with seafood and wild game. During trawling season, Matine went back to Pointe-aux-Chenes to get her summer shrimp. At 95, she told me when she turned 25 she thought she had lived half her life. At that time, most people she knew died early. She laughed and said, "I had no idea that you would come along."

Xavier's Room | **Bayou Terre-aux-Boeufs** | **2004**

Matine's oldest son, Xavier Verdin, at home in his room in their house on Bayou Road. He once shared his room with his three brothers, but as they grew up and moved out of the house, he remained—growing from a boy to an old man under the loving care of his mother. When I was a girl, Matine and my aunt Millie Cheramie explained to me that Xavier was a grown man, but his mind was similar to that of a five-year-old child. For many years, he was on medication that sedated him and induced a night owl pattern where he would sleep most of the day, wake at three in the afternoon for his coffee, and then stay awake all night watching *M*A*S*H*. When I was about 16, he quit taking the medicine and started going to church with my grandmother and taking care of the St. Bernard Catholic Cemetery. It was like he had awoken after years of functioning half-asleep.

In the 1980s, her hands were full when some oil and gas folks, making promises of fortune, said they wanted to put a right-of-way on our land. Matine told my dad, "You got to talk to them." It surprised him that she nominated him. He always said, "I don't have a pot to piss in or a window to throw it out of." Material things didn't matter to him. He met the businessmen in a hotel room, and they asked him to sign paperwork to come onto the land. He told them, "I'm not doing this"—probably not so politely. Shortly thereafter, they put the wells right on the other side of our property line. Black spots started appearing. Grass started dying in the yard. He told me that's what happens when they suck the oil away.

Joining Old Trail Routes

My parents met disco dancing at the Déjà Vu Lounge in the French Quarter of New Orleans. Reneé Michelle Neyrey was skinny and lanky like the Olive Oyl cartoon character. Raised on St. Roch Avenue in Gentilly, she was just 16. Two years before, her mom had died and she helped raise her two younger brothers. Her father's French Creole family lived on Esplanade Avenue at North Lopez. Her father's mother is said to be the first woman to work in a bank in New Orleans. She had a business school, spoke three languages, and was helping to raise some of my cousins. When her daughter-in-law died, she could only help so much.

My mom said my dad saved her life because she was in the wind—nobody really wanted her. He took her to Matine's house and they told her that she was of age. When my mom's brothers met my father, they asked him what he "was" and he told them, "I'm a saltwater nigga from Desire." And they quit asking questions.

A few years later, my mom said I was conceived after an August boat blessing and too much warm draft beer. I arrived as the baby cousin of the 14 grandchildren. My parents lived right next door to Matine in a trailer house. One of my first memories is being scolded for walking outside in the middle of the night to go see her when I was mad. My parents explained to me why I should be scared, but I wasn't.

Both Matine and my mother wanted my father to get a steady job and be "normal." All of my aunts and uncles had assimilated into broader American culture. My aunts married white men who were in the military. My uncles moved to Slidell and Kenner to live in the suburbs. But my dad preferred to live a seasonal life. He worked on the docks and as an air conditioning and refrigeration technician, but he would have preferred fishing, oystering, and shrimping. He liked swatting mosquitoes and watching the sunrise over the marsh. He loved the pirate life. Meanwhile, my mom was waiting tables by night, working at a bank by day, and selling Avon on the side. Sometimes my dad would leave on Friday and not come back until late Sunday, or Monday morning, when he had to go back to work after a weekend of gambling and partying in barrooms.

When I was two, my mom moved out and found a house in the Lower Ninth Ward. It was the early 1980s, and crack was hitting hard. Our house got robbed a couple of times. The public schools around our house were failing, and she knew that she wasn't going to be able to afford private schools. In 1984, she worked the New Orleans World's Fair, saved as much money as she could, and moved us to Pensacola, Florida, in time for me to start kindergarten.

Growing Up Together and Apart
St. Bernard and Pensacola | Late 1980s
Left: A polaroid with my dad, Herbert, in Matine's yard. *Right:*
My mom and me on the roof of our home on Pensacola Beach.

My father didn't take it well. He was heartbroken. He was installing a lot of air conditioning units in Section Eight housing being built in the Ninth Ward. He told me, "I went to the Ninth Ward because I wanted them to kill me, and then they made me family." He started hanging out with a bunch of Creoles and black folk in back-a-town around the Florida Avenue Canal. They used to call it Free-land because poor people could just go and build a little house for themselves next to the cypress swamp where Bayou Bienvenue ran toward Lake Borgne.

I was angry at my mom for moving us away from Louisiana. I felt disconnected in Pensacola; like I didn't belong. In hindsight, I can say to her, "Oh my God, Mom, thanks! You moved us to a barrier island, and I had a great education." She raised me on the beach with a lot of funky woolly-boogers looking to live on island time, but it was hard to adjust to the lack of diversity, Bible belt mentalities, and military presence in the area. I longed for the rest of my family. Every holiday, summer, and any other time I could manage, I returned to St. Bernard. I caught rides on small cargo planes, and with spring breakers, my uncle who was a hot shot driver, and friends of my mom's going to the New Orleans Jazz and Heritage Festival.

Matine's eldest daughter—my aunt Amelia "Millie" Cheramie—was the rock of the family. She handled most of Matine's banking and bills, and drove her to the grocery store. Added to these responsibilities was picking me up in Pensacola so I could come back to Matine. On the elevated I-10 interstate, we drove through Pascagoula, Biloxi, and Mobile before passing the *"Bienvenue a Louisiane"* sign at the state border. These place-names were originally the names of nations. The roads we traveled followed the high ground of natural ridges that traced precolonial trade routes. When my mom was able to drive part of the way, our meeting spot, the McDonald's off Exit 69 in Pascagoula, was near the birthplace of our ancestor, Touh-la-Bay. Like many of the mounds built by our ancestors around the Lower Mississippi River Valley, we do not know all of the stories of these places, but traces remain.

When I settled in at Matine's house, I looked forward to Sundays with all of my cousins. I ate three lunches as waves of people came through to visit. Sometimes my dad was around, other times he was AWOL and no one knew where he was. He didn't pay child support or tell me to do my homework—he was never a father figure in that kind of way—but he took me into the bottomland hardwood forests and the marsh, and told me, "Okay. This is it." What he meant was that this land was our real inheritance. My mother's family can trace their roots back to the founding of the French colony, but I didn't grow up feeling as connected to this part of our history.

Ici Repose (Here Rests) | **St. James Parish Cemetery** | **2019**

Next to the Mississippi River, the St. James Parish Catholic Cemetery was founded in 1750 and holds the remains of many of the original French colonists who founded Louisiana. Located on the Mississippi River between New Orleans and Baton Rouge, the Parish was named after one of my mother's ancestors, Jacques Nicholas Santiago Cantrelle. He came to Louisiana in 1720 with John Law's Company of the Indies. In 1729, he escaped death during the Natchez Revolt at Fort Rosalie, where almost all of the 150 French colonists were killed. When France ceded Louisiana to Spain, Jacques and his sons-in-law, Louis Judice and Nicolas Verret, received land grants north of New Orleans on the west bank of the Mississippi River in a place called Cabanocey, an indigenous name meaning "roosting place of wild ducks." The area remained predominantly indigenous until the arrival of Acadian exiles from Canada, who also received land grants from Spain.

Cantrelle Family Tomb | **St. James Parish Cemetery** | **2019**

In the Spanish census of 1766, many different indigenous tribes are documented in St. James Parish. The interactions between Cantrelle and the Houma bands in the area has been documented through correspondence between his sons-in-law, Judice and Verret, who were commanders in the government. In Judice's correspondence to his superior, he reports that a plantation owner on the east bank of the river is complaining that even though Houma Chief Calabe sold the "Houmas Claim" to him 10 years earlier, there are Indians on the property. In a 1783 record, natives are still living on the plantations: 58 on Judice's property, 17 on Verrett's, and 15 reported on Cantrelle's. Houma continue to live on Cantrelle's lands until the first decade of the 19th century.

Bayou Booray | **Pointe-aux-Chenes** | **2002**
Growing up, Anesie and Jane Verdin hosted family gatherings that often included all-day card games called Booray, serenaded with Cajun music. Everyone loved to play my father (*right*) when he would wear his sunglasses so they could see his hand reflected in his lenses.

Return to Yakni Chitto

Although Matine was based in St. Bernard, she made sure that Terrebonne remained an important anchor for us. We returned for the Blessing of the Boats in the spring, All Saints Day in November, and family reunions, weddings, and funerals. One family reunion in Pointe-aux-Chenes was at the Live Oak Baptist Church on the west side of the bayou. No beer was allowed on the premises. After a while, my dad started to get antsy and rallied for us to go across the bayou to visit Tunt Jeanne's daughter, Jane, and her husband Anesie Verdin. In search of a cold beer, we came up to a bunch of people gathered around a pile of freshly boiled shrimp on top of a makeshift plywood and sawhorse table, talking in Houma French. That memory stayed with me through my childhood. It was unlike other parts of the U.S. I had known. It felt like home.

Matine's best friend and sister-in-law Jeanne's house in Grand Bois was our main outpost in Terrebonne Parish.

Her house is located along the old Bayou Blue. Historically, this bayou was a much-traveled transportation route, but it had largely been forgotten and buried in the wake of water management infrastructures. Instead, many Houma families took an old logging canal, the St. Louis, from Pointe-aux-Chenes to Grand Bois. It was on higher ground and a safe place to go for hurricanes. We often stayed overnight with Jeanne before heading back to St. Bernard. Matine and I shared a double bed in one of the spare bedrooms. At dawn, I could hear those two talking in Houma French to each other in the kitchen, drinking their demitasse coffees that were black as oil and sweet as candy. The morning ritual was a prelude to church and long afternoons filled with family, an incredible meal, and a card game to follow.

In the 1960s, Highway 24 was constructed to create a shortcut between Bayou Terrebonne and Bayou Lafourche to Port Fourchon—the United States' largest

Grave Painting | **Bayou Terrebonne** | **2003**
Anesie Verdin paints the grave of my
great-grandmother, Celestine Verdin Roussell,
with tombstone paint, in Bisland Cemetery
along the banks of the Bayou Terrebonne.
Matine planned to be buried here with her
relatives. By the time she was 80, she had
made all her arrangements, down to the songs
she wanted played during her funeral service.
When she was 98, we went and picked out her
headstone, and she updated her plan to have her
wake in the old St. Bernard Catholic Church
and then caravan the coffin home to rest in the
Yakni Chitto.

Crawfish Lesson
Pointe-aux-Chenes | 2002
Clarice Friloux shares crawfish with Kailyn Verdin. In Houma legend, the *saktce-ho'ma* (red crawfish) is said to have gone to the bottom of the sea and built the land up for the people, animals, and plants to have a place to live. Clarice explains how eating seafood in South Louisiana is a major concern after the federal government's Resource Conservation and Recovery Act (RCRA) allowed a loophole for individual states to decide their own regulation of "oil field waste." Louisiana now labels material considered hazardous as nonhazardous. In the case of her community in Grand Bois, this waste is allowed to be disposed of and "treated" in a flood zone south of the Gulf Intracoastal Waterway.

deep-water oil port. Grand Bois saw a boom in business. Barrooms opened to cater to both the local community and the added oil field and ship-building traffic. In the spring of 1998, towards the end of my senior year in high school, I saw a *60 Minutes* special on CBS called "Town Under Siege." Grand Bois, this place I had visited my entire life, was at the center of a growing environmental justice movement related to the oil industry.

In 1980, Congress granted oil companies an exemption from regulations around hazardous waste removal, which had begun to prey on small communities in South Louisiana. A local company bought land 2,000 feet away from Grand Bois and built open air oil field waste pits. In 1994, Exxon brought waste from a treatment plant in Alabama containing benzene, xylene, hydrogen sulfide, and arsenic to Grand Bois. Men wearing protective clothing and masks dumped the waste into the pits, and a horrible smell overwhelmed the entire town. Many people started getting sick. My cousin, Clarice Friloux, brought a collective action case forward in *Clarice Friloux et al. v. Exxon Corp. and Campbell Wells Corp.*, which brought a small settlement, but not the full closure of the pits.

New Orleans

After graduation, my friends from Pensacola planned to attend college and join sororities and fraternities. This didn't seem like my path. On Christmas night of 1998, I was pointed in a different direction. On Lower Decatur Street in the French Quarter of New Orleans, I met Barry Kaiser at Maximo's, an Italian restaurant where Herman Leonard and other photographers often held court. Barry told me to come by his studio a few blocks away if I was interested in learning about his medium. For 30 years, he had been nesting in an old, third-floor attic apartment where sailors, sex workers, and Sicilian immigrants once resided. Every wall and nook was covered with stories. On my first afternoon assisting him, he photographed a fan dancer in the studio and a ballerina on the street. After our day together, I decided I wouldn't go to college. I moved back with Matine and started taking photographs.

Carnival Monkey
Frenchmen Street, New Orleans | 2000

To pay my bills, I got a job in New Orleans at a Kwik Kopy print shop working for a conservative Baptist, north Louisiana, retired school teacher, renaissance woman named Valentine Dyson. Her franchise was at 1716 St. Charles Avenue in an old Victorian building that had been Corrine Dunbar's home and restaurant. Drop ceilings and carpet disguised its former beauty.

I soon wrecked my car. Since I was unable to travel back and forth to Matine's every day, a Vietnam-vet friend of my mom's let me stay at his apartment across from Washington Square Park on Frenchmen Street in exchange for cleaning and checking in guests when he rented it out to weekend vacationers. On Frenchmen Street one afternoon, the owner of Café Brasil, Adgenor "Adé" Salgado, was standing in front of his building wearing a maroon suit and smoking a cigar. He pointed at me, "You! Come work for me!"

"I'm 19! I can't!"

"What? Five o'clock! Friday!" And then he fired me a few months later for how I dressed.

I protested, "Adé, it's fucking cold, man! It's twenty degrees in here, and it's Hip Hop Night. I got a bomber jacket on. What do you want from me?"

"You dress like a boy."

"I don't want to work here anyway! I told you I was only 19."

In the summer of 1999, I rented my first apartment in the Lower Garden District on Euterpe Street, named after the Greek goddess of music, song, and dance. The surrounding streets were named after the other eight muses. Most of the big, old town homes were boarding houses. Coliseum Square was a resting place for homeless until they could check into one of the many shelters and halfway houses nearby: New Orleans Mission, Ozanam Inn, or Bridge House.

My dad called Matine's home, but he was a rambling man. He lived in the city, up the road in Chalmette, out of his van, with his girlfriends, on oyster boats. When the Temptations' "Papa Was a Rollin' Stone" came on a radio, he always said, "That's my song!" He disappeared sometimes. We didn't always know a hundred percent where he was, but when he was around, he took me on drives to visit fishing villages where the roads end in St. Bernard Parish or up the road to school me on navigating the city.

In our shortcuts through back-a-town, he introduced me to his friend, John Taylor. John told me, "Everybody called your dad Julio, but I knew he wasn't a Mexican. I knew he was from the Parish. I was going into the Bayou Bienvenue swamp and bringing out garfish, and your dad was always coming up from down the road selling shrimp, coons, or turtle to all the Creoles who lived in the Lower Ninth Ward." Both my dad and John were wild salesmen who could see the truth. If you passed them in the street, maybe you wouldn't think twice, but they recognized real, simple beauty from the freedom they found in that wildness. Their spirits reflected the wisdom of *les sauvages*.

The Keepers of the Bayou | **Lower Ninth Ward, New Orleans** | **1999**
Herbert "Julio" Verdin and John "Red" Taylor in the Lower Ninth Ward.

Two Ways of Looking | **St. Thomas Public Housing Development, New Orleans** | **1990s**
A St. Thomas resident watches Elizabeth Rappaport photographing her courtyard.
Photograph courtesy of Elizabeth Rappaport.

I had my mother's blue collar work ethic in me. For five years, I kept a steady job working for Valentine as a printer's apprentice. Some days I felt like a little doggie in the window, watching the world go by—people getting on and off the streetcar, the same homeless folks walking in and out of the Burger King next door—but I met people from all corners of uptown society: schoolteachers, writers, architects, and lawyers.

On Euterpe Street, Elizabeth Rappaport and I shared the same landlord, Mrs. Polly Watts. A documentary photographer, for two years Elizabeth had covered the Bosnian War before finding her way to New Orleans to work on a story about the Abstract Bookshop. Located in the Lower Garden District near the St. Thomas Public Housing Development, it was a home for people battling addictions and homelessness. She taught me that you can't ignore what you know.

Elizabeth had the most incredible photo book library and in her backyard was a darkroom full of paper and chemicals. She told me, "Get in there. Go make pictures!" And that was our barter: I worked in the darkroom in exchange for taking care of the cats while she was away traveling for work or escaping the summer doldrums. She let me borrow her 35mm Nikon FE2 with a wide angle lens. I took it with me when I went down to Terrebonne Parish to be with my family.

Carol and Jane Popping Heads | **Pointe-aux-Chenes** | **2001**
Jane helping her daughter, Carol Rodriguez, prepare for dinner. Carol is one of the best cooks down Bayou Pointe-aux-Chenes. Shrimp ettouffee, boulettes, and fried soft-shell crabs are just a few of her specialties. She can pop shrimp heads two at a time, and pick up a sack of oysters with one hand.

I planned to use photography as a tool to raise awareness about the environmental injustices they were facing. Instead, I found myself following the children to the edge of the old forest, sitting on Tunt Jeanne's front porch with elders, or taking up Jane and Anesie on their open-door policy over in Pointe-aux-Chenes. As family stopped by for unannounced visits, strangers cruising the bayou bought freshly caught hard or soft crabs right out of the water. Crab fishermen stopped by to purchase catfish heads from Anesie to bait their crab traps. Their eldest daughter, Carol, and I share the same birthday and have a cosmic sisterhood. I used to spend a lot of time with her and her children, Allison and Leonardo.

Mother & Daughter Down the Bayou | **Bayou Pointe-aux-Chenes** | **2003**
Carol and Allison Rodriguez along the bayouside. Carol moved to Houma after marrying Santos, an Aztec/Mexican oyster fisherman. Although her house is in Houma, Carol is most at home down the bayou. She has raised her kids surrounded by family, speaking to them in Houma French, and feeding them the traditional way with fresh seafood.

Matine and Jeanne's Homeland | **Pointe-aux-Chenes** | **2000**
The best friends return to the place where they grew up. To the south of where they are standing,
the fresh water and brackish estuaries of Terrebonne Bay lead out to the Gulf of Mexico.

Matine's Map | **Pointe-aux-Chenes** | **2000**

On the Pointe, Matine showed us where my great-grandmother, Celestine, buried her husband under a live oak tree *(On the left page of this spread, it is on the right)*. After he died from yellow fever, she pulled his body into a pirogue and rowed, all alone, across Bayou Pointe-aux-Chenes. This tree is one of the only surviving live oaks down the bayou. The others have died from salt water intrusion.

In the fall of 2000, Anesie took Jeanne and Matine on a three-mile boat ride from where the Pointe-aux-Chenes road ends to "the Pointe," the ridge where they grew up. They were shocked at the changes to the landscape. I remember thinking that the feeling that swept over them would never happen to me. At least, not so dramatically.

In the chapter that follows, Anesie and Jane share their life stories in Terrebonne Parish. A five-time throat cancer survivor, Anesie has lost his voice. As we were putting the book together, I read him back the words he can no longer speak.

these are the good old days
and a people you can get behind

the treasures that they find
hang in the air; sublime
rusty boat motors
moldy green nets
and the smell of crawfish boiling in
a great big pot
          spanish moss
and the young kids toss their hair
when the jetskis
          go spurtin' by

—from "in pointe-aux-chenes"
Raymond "Moose" Jackson

Morning Sun & an Onion | **Grand Bois** | **2000**
While watching Jeanne Verdin at her kitchen sink one
Sunday morning, I realized the unique technique she
used to slice an onion was the same meditative precision
I had witnessed in the hands of Matine.

PART III
CROSSING TIME

Jane Verdin: I grew up in Grand Bois, between Bourg and Larose in Terrebonne Parish. My mama, Jeanne, has Alzheimer's and she always talks about her house down the bayou in Pointe-aux-Chenes. She asks me what she's doing in Grand Bois, why they won't come get her. I said, "Well, I guess love brought you over here."

Hot Cocoa and Fried Crepe | **Grand Bois** | **2004**
Jane Verdin with her mother, Jeanne Verdin. Only Tunt Jeanne's front porch could compete with the kitchen as the best place in the neighborhood to gather, but when hot cocoa and fried *crepe* (fry bread) were on the fire, there was no contest.

Enola Roussell Dardar (1929–2008) | **Grand Bois** | **2004**

Although the Houma diaspora is spread around south Louisiana, many people still come back to visit the bayous of Terrebonne and Lafourche Parishes. Here is one of Matine's sisters, Enola Roussell Dardar, in her Sunday best at Tunt Jeanne's house. She lived in Lafitte, Louisiana.

Marcellin Roussell (1942–2016) on Jeanne's Porch | **Grand Bois** | **2004**
Jeanne Verdin's front porch was made for long afternoon visits filled with coffee, a little sweet treat, and a rhythm between songs traded in the old Houma French and long silences filled in by cars and trucks flying by on the interstate.

Jeanne Verdin (1918-2019) at Bisland Cemetery | **Bayou Terrebonne** | **2001**

Every October, in preparation for All Saints' and All Souls' days, my family made our ritual pilgrimage from St. Bernard to wash and paint the graves of my great-grandparents and grandfather Toussaint. At the graveyard in Bourg, we often met up with family members washing other graves. When our work was done, we went for a visit in Grand Bois to pick ripe satsumas and say hello to our cousins before heading back to St. Bernard.

Leonardo Rodriguez at Bisland Cemetery | **Bayou Terrebonne** | **2001**
Goldenrod blooms at the end of fall. Leonardo holds a wand of this special plant on All Saints' Day in Bisland, which is surrounded by a sugarcane field, a little patch of bottomland hardwoods, and a highway following the old bayou.

Tunt Jeanne's Back Porch | **Grand Bois** | **2000**
Jesuit journals from colonial times note that the Houma
revered their chickens as sacred animals who lived in
their homes, and that they refused to kill them. Although
these traditions have gone by the wayside, chickens and
roosters are still very much a part of Houma life. They
wander freely in yards when not safely tucked away in
their pens. At Tunt Jeanne's, they wander over the open
land that used to be Bayou Blue before it was cut off from
headwaters and filled in.

Dillon Verdin and Chicken | **Grand Bois** | **2000**
Dillon Verdin had a special relationship with this particular chicken and was able to get her to
perch on his shoulder. Not all Houma chickens are this friendly.

Anesie Verdin: When I was growing up, we had a ridge of land south of Pointe-aux-Chenes we called Isle Falla. My grandfather on my father's side was camping there. If they'd go in, they have to paddle the pirogues by hand all the way to Golden Meadow. Then an old fella down here, he had a little sailboat. Later on, they had some small boat with some engine to go back and forth.

Over on Isle Jean Charles, they didn't have no road. The only transportation they had was by water. After our people left from the Isle Falla, we'd go by boat to see them in Golden Meadow. Our transportation was by water, too.

We started fishing and we kept on fishing. When my daddy went shrimping, they had to pick everything by hand. Since I was young—maybe five years old—I started following him and got into his footprint that I kept until I knew what to do. Early on, we got some boats, so we fished by ourselves. We go swap a chicken or some fish for some rice, coffee, or sugar.

Anesie Verdin on His Boat | **Pointe-aux-Chenes** | **2000**
There is always work to be done when you are a fisherman—nets to be mended, engines to be worked on, just to start with—but Anesie always makes time to take family members on long rides in his boat down the bayou. One of my favorite memories is going out with him at sunrise on the opening day of shrimp season. We dropped the trawl boards to drag the water bottoms for *fruit de mer* (seafood), and I took a nap on his bow, rocked to sleep with the hum of the motor.

Veronica's Net | **Pointe-aux-Chenes** | **2000**
Veronica Verdin, Anesie and Jane's youngest daughter, showing the boys
how to cast a net properly to catch fish out of Bayou Pointe-aux-Chenes.

Chris's Net | **Pointe-aux-Chenes** | **2002**

Chris Verdin, Anesie and Jane's youngest son, repairs a net used for shrimping. All of their children were born and raised on along Bayou Pointe-aux-Chenes, but they have not followed the footsteps of their father. With competition from foreign markets and the price of diesel so high, it is hard to make a full-time living from commercial fishing. Some of Anesie's sons and grandsons still shrimp during time off from their other jobs.

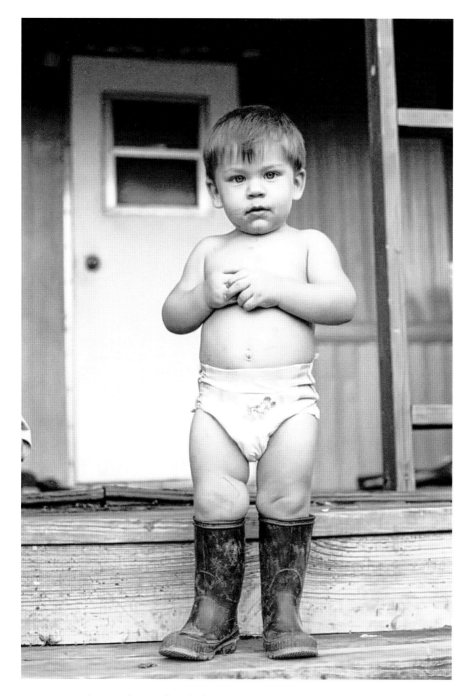

Baby Brynan's Boots | **Grand Bois** | *2002*

Brynan, one of Anesie and Jane Verdin's youngest grandsons, wearing baby shrimp boots: a necessary step to learn how the lines of land and water are constantly changing. For the first few years of his life, Brynan lived on family property in Grand Bois before moving to Pointe-aux-Chenes.

Anesie: The Billiot family, related to us, was living in Marrero in Jefferson Parish, and that old boy had an old truck that come down and pick up the crabs. They were selling fish for 10 to 12 cents a pound; the crab for like 25 cents a bushel. Now, a lot of times, it's 25 dollars, maybe 50 dollars a bushel of crab!

That old boy built a little shed down here. He got a little bit bigger and bigger. Then they got another guy who came down. He build another place by the bayou. Every day competition, you see. He only bought shrimp, but that other fella from Marrero, you could come with some fish, some shrimp, some crab. You can go trapping, he'd buy your fur and all.

For trapping season, we wouldn't go set a trap over here. We'd move somewhere else. We might go in Plaquemines Parish, St. Bernard Parish. We would leave in October, we might come back home back in March. Two to three places that we went, we had to travel by boat. They didn't have no road. We had a boat to row to the camp. We needed grocery or something, we had to come to the front and buy our grocery, then go back to the camp.

They had an old boy across the bayou who had an old car. He was like a cab driver. He'd take us to town and back. Man, it was comfortable riding in a car! I remember the first car that my daddy owned was a 1957 Ford. We didn't have no road on this side of the bayou. We had to cross the bayou by pirogue to get to the car when want to go to town somewhere.

Boat Blessing: Family Fleet | **Pointe-aux-Chenes** | **1999**

In Louisiana, we have two shrimp seasons. In the spring, the shrimp are brown, and in late summer and early fall, they are white. Down Bayou Pointe-aux-Chenes, the annual Blessing of the Fleet usually occurs the Sunday before the May season opens. The local priest leads the procession of boats and fishermen, blessing the waters and all those on the bayouside. He prays for a bountiful season, and for the safety of our fishermen and fisherwomen. Boats loaded down with family and friends fall in line behind the main boat. My great-uncle Sidney's family boat follows the procession out to Lake Felicity to meet up with others to welcome in the season.

Bayouside Boil | **Pointe-aux-Chenes** | **2000**
Ernie Verdin's silhouette depicts a typical afternoon on the bayouside of Pointe-aux-Chenes, the
epicenter of the community: a place where seafood is sold, cooked, and eaten fresh off the boat.
A place to boil a couple pounds of shrimp caught fresh that morning.

Ernie Verdin and a Flat of Soft-shell Crabs
Pointe-aux-Chenes | 2002

The Verdin family have holding tanks set up for "buster" blue crabs getting ready to shed their shells. Tending to soft shell crabs requires a round-the-clock watch. Every two hours, someone has to check to see if a crab has molted. If they have, the crabs have to be pulled out of the water before re-hardening sets in.

Indian Schoolhouse and Kitchen | **Pointe-aux-Chenes** | **1999**
Until the late 1960s, Terrebonne and Lafourche parish schools were segregated into "white" and "colored" schools. Methodists and Baptists established missionary schools for Houma children down Bayou Pointe-aux-Chenes.

Jane: In Golden Meadow, they had an Indian school, but that was the elementary school. When Houma had to go to high school, they couldn't mess with the white people. But at that time, the colored people wasn't allowed to go in the white schools, either. Martin Luther King, Jr., opened the doors for the colored and the Indians.

Anesie: Pointe-aux-Chenes had a little school across the bayou at the Baptist Church.

Jane: The Baptist Church was named Live Oak.

Anesie: And then they moved a little school from Larose on a barge. The people from the Isle de Jean Charles and Pointe-aux-Chenes would go to that school.

Jane: When they'd have to go to high school, they'd go to Larose, but not many of them made it.

Anesie: Not many made it. No.

Jane: When I went to school, I couldn't speak English, not at all! I want to speak French, yeah. I have to learn how to speak English before I could learn anything in school! I failed the first grade.

Anesie: When my daddy got sick, I quit school in ninth grade to help him out. We still spoke French to our children. Some of our grandchildren understand us, but they respond in English.

Lil Black Chicken | **Pointe-aux-Chenes** | **2000**
When Allison Rodriguez was little, her grandfather, Anesie Verdin, used to call her *la ti poulet neg* (the little black chicken).

Allison Rodriguez: I was born in 1997 in Houma. I am Latina and Indian. Whenever my teachers would hand out the Indian papers, I would never get them. I thought, "I am Native American, why am I not getting any of this?" Then I learned when we had papers sent home from school, my mom would not put anything under "race" because she wanted me to do it. She listed me as "Other" because she wanted me to decide. I decided I am not an other. I'm both.

Carol Verdin Rodriguez | **Grand Bois** | **2001**
Anesie and Jane's oldest daughter, mother to Leonardo and Allison, at Marie's Bar.

Jane: I met Anesie at my father's bar in Grand Bois. The law didn't care too much for the people way down in the woods, so I was maybe 15 years old when I started working there. It's called Marie's Bar now.

Elta "Tot" Verdin Billiot (1943–2002) at Marie's | **Grand Bois** | **2001**

Tot was born, raised, and died in Grand Bois. In this photograph, she is sitting behind the bar at the establishment started by her father, Evence Verdin, and run for many years by her sister, Marie. At one time there were four or five barrooms in Grand Bois, but by the late 1990s, only Marie's survived. When the barroom closed after the storms of 2008, some of our relatives felt like orphans with nowhere to go. Marie's was more than a barroom; it was a home place for many where birthday parties and anniversaries were celebrated, or a place to relax to the old chanky-chank on the jukebox after a long day of work.

Pool Sharks at Marie's | **Grand Bois** | **2003**
My father loved to play pool, cards, dice, bet on horses, and spent a fair amount of time circling cockfights, too. He was known for his ability to make the shot on the pool table or while out on a hunt.

Buster Naquin (1944–2019) at Marie's | **Grand Bois** | **2003**

When a blue crab starts to shed its shell to make room for new growth, we call it a "buster." Buster "Buck" Naquin, a lifelong resident of Pointe-aux-Chenes and crabber, used to drive to Grand Bois every day to drink coffee, play cards, and occasionally sit in to open beers at Marie's Bar.

Morgan Chaisson (1964–2007) at Marie's Bar | **Grand Bois** | **2003**
Morgan was born in Grand Bois and lived there all his life. He had sparkly blue eyes and never wore shoes. The whole town knew him. Every day, he walked the highway from his mama's house to Marie's Bar. He wasn't really fond of having his picture taken, but one December day, we made a series of images together as we wandered around the bar and inside my Tunt Jeanne's yard.

Morgan and Can Savings | **Grand Bois** | **2004**
Morgan used to make a little money on the side collecting cans at Marie's Bar and banking them in Tunt Jeanne's side yard.
A caretaker of sorts for Jeanne, he was willing to lend a hand whenever he could.

Reflection | **Grand Bois** | **2004**

Grand Bois was historically the high ground where relatives from Pointe-aux-Chenes further evacuated for safety. Land loss, subsidence, sea-level rise, and hard levee infrastructures built to reduce risks in other communities have now made Grand Bois more vulnerable to the storm surges. In 2004, I rode out Hurricane Ivan in Pensacola. A few weeks later, that same storm returned to the Atlantic, circled back into the Gulf of Mexico, and struck south Louisiana as a little tropical depression while I was visiting relatives in Grand Bois. I took this photograph the morning after the storm had rolled through. We woke to Tunt Jeanne's house surrounded by floodwaters.

Jeanne Verdin the Morning after the Storm | **Grand Bois** | **2004**
My cousins said the storm had followed me. Tunt Jeanne was quiet, looking out the
window in disbelief at the water surrounding the island that was her home.

Captain Pete | **Grand Bois** | **2004**
Brynan Verdin riding through the floodwaters brought in by a storm. I, too, felt like a little kid, wandering about the yard fascinated at how the water covered the community. And then I remembered that if the town had flooded, the oil field waste pits had flooded, too.

New Frontier | **Grand Bois** | **2004**
Brent Verdin converted an aluminum box, used to hold shrimp, into a boat to
paddle around the yard after a tropical storm surge submerged his lawn.

Graduation | **Grand Bois** | **2005**

A few months before Hurricanes Katrina and Rita, I had the opportunity to photograph Brent Verdin's graduation. Even after decades of integration, high school graduation and college enrollment rates for Houma students remain below average. Twenty-two percent of Houma adults have not graduated high school.

What the Future Holds | **Grand Bois** | **2005**
Shortly after graduating, Brent decided to look for other opportunities outside of Grand Bois. Instead of following in his father's and uncles' footsteps to work as a welder in oil fields and sugar refineries, he sought out another path and moved to Baton Rouge before eventually making his way to Texas.

Cockfighting on a Sunday Afternoon | **Grand Bois** | **2006**
After the storms of 2005, Sunday cock fights brought a diverse spectrum of peoples from surrounding bayous together: Houma, Cajuns, Creoles, Mexicans and Vietnamese all gathered in backyards with their foul and money in their hands. In 2008, Louisiana became the last state in the nation to ban cock fighting.

Clarice Friloux after Ike | **Grand Bois** | **2008**

After Hurricane Ike, Clarice rode a flat boat from the dry island of her sister's home to the high ground along Highway 24. Although her community was flooded and without electricity, she was also helping other Houma communities further south as well. Down in Dulac, she unloaded a semi-truck full of ice for trawlers to save their catch and for families to keep their food from spoiling. She continued to facilitate recovery logistics long after the floodwaters subsided.

Anesie at Home | **Pointe-aux-Chenes** | **2008**

Anesie Verdin standing on a wooden plank that leads to the staircase. A life vest is wrapped around the tree. To adapt to higher storm surges, Anesie raised his home another eight feet since this photograph was taken. Communities across the coast of Louisiana are currently facing how they "remain and reclaim," or retreat to higher grounds further inside levee risk reduction systems, and leave their bayouside ways of life behind.

Pirogue Ride to High Ground | **Pointe-aux-Chenes** | **2008**
Jane Verdin catches a ride to get to the dry road that passes in front of her house along Bayou Pointe-aux-Chenes.

Allison: When a storm hits in Pointe-Aux-Chenes, the water is going to rise, the wind is going to get really rough. On the levee, there are gas cans and ice chests full of water and food. Afterwards, "Okay, it's time to do it again." Start cleaning, picking things up. There's water everywhere. As kids, it's fun. You just go play in the water, ride in the boats, go find things that have floated away. We never looked at it like it was a horrible thing. We knew together we could pick up the pieces, and go back to normal.

Boys Bailing Floodwater | **Pointe-aux-Chenes** | **2008**
Justin Verdin, Leonardo Rodriguez, and Beau Verdin became accustomed to the cycle of
storms washing into their homes and disrupting their lives. The truth is, we no longer
need a hurricane for coastal communities to flood. All we need is a south wind to blow a
little too hard, a little too long. With the erosion of the barrier islands, the Gulf of Mexico
can easily roll in.

Ghost Forest | **Pointe-aux-Chenes** | **2009**

When Matine was a girl, the bayou was lined with live oaks and hackberry trees with pecan groves and prairie. Now where she harvested pecans, my cousins fish for crabs.

Anesie: The waterways are still the same, but they wider now. A lot of the canals we have, they didn't have that when my daddy was trawling. They only have the main canal in the back. Now there are three different pipeline canals, and a couple canals that they cut to put some rigs. It's just canals cut through and through.

When we got married, we had the islands and we had the trees. In the 1990s, we started losing the islands in Terrebonne Bay. All them islands washed away with all them storms. That's when it started eroding. They used to have some nice trees way down there. It make us feel bad that all our trees over here are gone.

They are talking about us having to move, but to go crabbing, shrimping, we have our boat right here. We jump in the boat, take off. If we move somewhere else, we'd have to jump in the truck, or car, and come down here. You'd have the expense of your car, and the expense of where to put your boat. Instead of building levees, they should redo them islands down there to break the water.

Anesie Verdin and Granddaughter, Allison Rodriguez | **Pointe-aux-Chenes** | **2008**

Allison: My dad is a commercial fisherman. He oystered for a living, which he did do good for himself. Now he has boats where guys go work for him. My grandpa went trawling until he couldn't do it anymore. When I was younger, I would go with him. We'd leave when it was still dark and I remember thinking to myself, "How can you see? How do you know where you to go?"

But he's been doing it all of his life. He knows where to go. He knows where not to pass where they have sand bars and oyster reefs. You have to know the bayou like he did to work in this place. Another thing, he'd tell us where we're shrimping now they used to have so much land. It just goes to show, in one person's lifetime, so many things could change.

The price and the seafood isn't as plentiful as it used to be. You have to start looking to do other things if you are young. My cousin thought he could go crabbing, but that's not something you can count on. He's just a few years older than me. But I don't think it's about the money for him. It's something that we grew up doing. In the future, if you want to do it, it may have to be a hobby. When you are growing up, you think you will have everybody forever and you just won't. You think you will have the land, the water, but you won't. My kids won't be able to do what I used to do with my grandpa, and it hurts.

Why am I crying? These are involuntary tears!

When I think about it, I have to wonder, "If you see something causing a problem to somebody's way of life, why wouldn't you stop?" For us, you can't put a price on it. I don't want to live here on the bayou full-time because of the floods, but there is always the coming back to this place. Especially in the fall, you want to be at a bayouside, just sitting, because the weather is beautiful. And it's comforting. I want to be out in the country.

On the Surface | **Pointe-aux-Chenes** | **2010**

In the summer of 2010, British Petroleum's Deepwater Horizon drilling disaster induced a black tide of crude oil, which was soon followed by the unlawful release of the toxic chemical Corexit to sink it to the bottom. Shrimp season opened three days after the spill began, but they couldn't get the ocean floor to stop bleeding. Just before they closed the waters to fishing, we got a chance to go out for a night to skim on top of the water for shrimp using butterfly nets. First cousins Beau Verdin and Leonardo Rodriguez pick through the bycatch, separating the shrimp from the little fish, eels, crabs, and other sea life caught in the net.

the elders said, "granddaughter,
tradition bids us here
each year, where the children
swim over the bones of our houses
left long ago
where stood our land.
our gardens bloomed
where this water flows."

but this year
the children swim
over homes of their own

—from "ancestor poem"
by Raymond "Moose" Jackson

Cry You One: Palmetto Hut/Skirt | **40 Arpent Canal, St. Bernard Parish** | **2013**
Melisa Cardona took this photograph of me on top of the geodesic dome that we transformed into a palmetto hut for the ArtSpot and Mondo Bizarro production of *Cry You One*.

PART IV
ART, LOVE, & THE LOUP GAROU

Mark Krasnoff | **The Coffin Box Project** | **2007**
On All Souls' Day, I began sorting through the collection of plastic post-Katrina yard signs Krasnoff and I had
found around greater Bulbancha (New Orleans metro area), advertising everything from mold remediation
to legal representation for residents seeking oil spill compensation. I built a series of "coffin boxes" out of the
recycled signs. This photo collage is from the inside of Krasnoff's coffin box.

The Loup Garou

Monique: In South Louisiana, we live on a power point of our planet. A place where water comes to be purified. A place where 1,000-year-old cypress trees once grew. A place where fish still come to spawn and birds to nest. A place close to the Gulf of Mexico, but where, as the old people used to say, "sweet water" could still be found that was fresh and good to drink.

There is no sweet water down the bayou in Terrebonne Parish anymore.

I've been trying to make sense of the strange beauty left here; the magic that is entangled in the ugliest underbelly of a plantation economy surrendered to the petro-chemical industry. Against this landscape, I see my cousins coming back to Pointe-aux-Chenes on the weekends, and my *jardin sauvage* on Bayou Road. I see indigenous and *metis* people reclaiming New Orleans' original name, Bulbancha. I remind myself of Matine's story of her aunt who lived in Plaquemines and still crossed the Mississippi River every day in a pirogue. I see connections of unexpected, non-coincidental, life-affirming experiences that fuse the stories of our ancestors with our hopes and prayers for a better future.

On a cold December night in 2003, I had one of these experiences. With the sole of my boot disconnecting and flapping with every step, I ended up sliding around on the dance floor of an old warehouse turned-club in New Orleans with Mark Krasnoff—a stranger who became my

Mark Krasnoff | **New Orleans** | **2002**
Portrait of Krasnoff in a puppet and
human staging of the play "Amadeus."
He played the role of composer Antonio
Salieri, the rival of Wolfgang Amadeus
Mozart. Photograph by Herman Leonard.

love, collaborator, and best friend. I was 23 years old. He had just turned 40 and recently divorced.

Krasnoff introduced himself as a "Cajun, Choctaw Jew" from Ville Platte, a small town in southwest Louisiana north of Opelousas. Our families had similar experiences with French. Like Jane and Anesie, his mother's generation was punished for speaking it at school and, in turn, many people never taught their children. It wasn't until he left home to attend the University of Lafayette that he began to reclaim the language. While his grandmother was on her deathbed, he practiced with her until her spirit passed. Later, he worked in Quebec with director André Forcier, which added an edge of Montreal to his Cajun roots.

When we met, I was struggling to express what I was doing with photography. Where I grew up, people thought activists were both naive and radical. Similarly, coming from a blue-collar background, calling yourself an "artist" was dismissed as pompous and ungrounded in others' realities. When I showed Krasnoff the images of my family, he was supportive—not just of the work, but in helping me find a community to share it with. He took me around the city and introduced me to key characters who were part of his spiritual family cosmology. He was

like, "Okay, Verdin, here are your people. They are going to love you. You are going to love them." And he was right. They changed my life.

Kathy Randels, Director of ArtSpot Productions: I met Krasnoff through the theater scene in New Orleans in the late 1990s. We had a talent crush on each other. He was older than me, wiser. We caught up whenever we saw each other. I used to run into him on Frenchmen Street a lot—everyone went there in the late 1990s, dodging the roaches and the nutria rats to enjoy the booze, dancing, and conversation at Café Brasil. Krasnoff was a friendly, open, excited-by-life man. You always knew it would be a good conversation when he was out. A born performer, entertainer, audience captivator.

Monique: His magic was his curiosity. People felt comfortable enough with him to tell him the secrets of their lives. When I brought him home, he made Matine laugh. He knew how to hang out for long afternoons while everyone was cooking. She loved that he liked to talk French with her friends, even though his tongue was more of what they would call "pretty French." On her 90th birthday, we accompanied her on a journey down Bayou Pointe-aux-Chenes. As we left the Parish, my father drank Busch beers

Matine's House | **Bayou Terre-aux-Beoufs** | **2006**

Hurricane Katrina pushed an 11-foot storm surge through our house in St. Bernard Parish. Matine, along with my father, uncle Xavier, and cousin Mike, were able to paddle out in pirogues. Matine was never one to ask for her picture be to taken, but in early 2006, when we returned to our home, she told me to take her picture in front of her house. She wanted people to see what that hurricane left behind in its wake.

In the months after the hurricane, she lived in suburban exile on the Westbank of the Mississippi, but every chance she got, she returned to her devastated home to sift through what could be salvaged. She pulled out her cast iron pots and made a fire outside to clean them, found her demitasse collection unbroken, and, in the armoire where the old photos used to be, she pulled out a jar of dimes, quarters, and pennies she had stashed away.

as he told stories to help get Krasnoff oriented. Laughing and distracted, I got pulled over making an illegal left turn. As my dad hid his beer under the seat behind his aunt's dress, Krasnoff's advice to the other elders was for nobody to speak English. When we finally made it to La Pointe, Jane made a feast of fried crabs and Anesie took us all on a boat ride back to the center of Matine's childhood. As I was taking photographs of my family, Krasnoff began to film them.

Soon, I moved into his house next to the cemetery on Adams Street in uptown New Orleans. We decided to create a documentary film. We hadn't gotten very far when Hurricane Katrina hit. The national media followed how the storm surge inundated the city, but less attention was given to how it had pushed through Plaquemines and St. Bernard Parishes through the Mississippi River Gulf Outlet—a man-made shipping canal that ran from the

After the Teardown | **Bayou Terre-aux-Boeufs** | **2006**
Photograph Mark Krasnoff took of Matine and me standing
by the remains of our home.

Gulf to the Lower Ninth Ward's Industrial Canal. It caused
catastrophic damage along the way. When we returned to
Matine's home, it was unrecognizable. An 11-foot water-
line wrapped around the house, and there was a major oil
spill in a residential neighborhood just up the road. In spite
of my resistance, Krasnoff turned the camera around on
me. There is a scene in our film, *My Louisiana Love,* where
he challenges me to express what I am witnessing. I'm
sitting at the kitchen table on the verge of tears, wanting
to return to my family's rituals of comfort and be left alone
to drink my coffee.

We were lost in the endless emptiness; in how a place
that once was your city could become such an other
kind of space. In the neutral grounds all around the city,
the insides of homes were mountains of garbage. Before
Katrina hit, people were not talking on a regular basis
about the benefits of healthy wetlands. There was not the
same consciousness of land loss. When folks came home to
flood lines above their heads, the learning curve rose. I had
heard of "global warming" before, but it seemed distant.
We didn't have the language to call things by their names.
We weren't able to say, "Oh, yeah, this is just life in the
times of the Anthropocene."

say goodnight to the *fais-do-do*
y'all been dancing
when you should have been workin

is this the way that it's all gonna go?
let them oilmen come to drink our blood
while the land disappears beneath our feet?

say goodnight to the crawfish boil
and great green beards of moss

the egret, so silent
in his endless toil

to the blessings of the fleet
say *bonne nuit*
to our culture, *la belle langue*

we just gonna dance
to the end of the song
til all that's left is the
fleur de lys
Le Vieux Drapeau

cheap nostalgia, flooded prose
pack your life into the pirogue, *ma mére*
it's out to sea we go

—Raymond "Moose" Jackson,
The Loup Garou: A Lunar Cycle

Xavier Verdin (1934-2017), Keeper of the Cemetery | **Bayou Terre-aux-Boeufs** | **2006**

Xavier never talked about their experience during the hurricane, but Matine said when they passed the cemetery after being picked up by neighbors in a motorboat, she couldn't see the tops of the tombs. My father flagged down the boat and asked that they ferry his elderly mother and brother to the fishing fleet tied up inside St. Bernard's Violet Canal. My father and cousin stayed behind When the surge of water and weather began to calm down, they paddled out to look for a better boat than the old pirogue they had. That's when they found a floating coffin and decided they had to tow it back to the church and tie it up. My dad swore the name on the coffin was one of his old schoolteachers—the mean one.

The State of Louisiana established the "Road Home" program for owners of flooded homes to get back on their feet. Matine signed up for her house to be bulldozed so she could buy a baby double-wide trailer to set up on her property. The St. Bernard Parish demo crew never came. Instead, my cousin Mike and a friend came over with some heavy machinery and tore down the cypress house. We showed up the next day to find its guts sitting in our front yard; a pile of trash waiting to be hauled away.

One day, my dad showed up at our house on Adams Street, looking ill and moving slow. I demanded he go to the hospital. He told me to take him to Charity, which, at that time, was a triage set up inside a former department store next to the Superdome. We learned his liver was failing. He had probably contracted hepatitis C in the 1970s from IV drug use. On top of that, he was a heavy drinker. The storm pushed him over the edge. With my grandmother's house demolished, his frame of reference, as well as the network

Xavier after Katrina in the St. Bernard Catholic Cemetery | **Bayou Terre-aux-Boeufs** | **2006**
After the storm, Xavier returned to caring for the old St. Bernard Catholic Cemetery. In the afternoon, he took long walks to check on things, and left special rocks on the tombs for those who had gone before. He always closed the gates before sunset. The cemetery was severely damaged by Katrina's storm surge.

of people who orientated his life—from the docks down the road to his friends back-a-town in the Ninth Ward—were gone. He died on June 14, 2006.

Kathy: After Katrina, my theater company started working on *Beneath the Strata/Disappearing*, a piece that we had been planning for a couple of years about coastal land loss in southeast Louisiana. At an artist residency at A Studio in the Woods, I imagined an all-women play. Glen Pitre, a filmmaker who comes from a Cajun family in Cut-Off—not far from Pointe-aux-Chenes—came out to visit us. He said where he came from in Terrebonne Parish, folks keep the waterlines on their houses not only because they are hard to clean off, but to remind them of the impermanence of this place. The power of *les ouragans* (the hurricanes) were more powerful than the *loup garou*, the werewolf that children hear stories about at bedtime.

there's an edge zone between
water and land
monster and man
love and lust; blood and rust
righteous anger and
blind carnal rage
that's the *territoire* of the Loup Garou
on the savage bayou
the leeward side of the moon…

–Raymond "Moose" Jackson,
The Loup Garou: A Lunar Cycle

Kathy: I thought, "An all-women piece needs a foil, just one strong shot of testosterone." A Loup Garou who could walk this fine line: intoxicating to those who are drunk with him, despicable to those who aren't—the ones who have had to clean up after him. But when he's in his high, and he's taking you with him on a long ride towards pure freedom, he's the sexiest thing alive. I asked Krasnoff to take on the role.

Monique: But he said he couldn't do it.

Kathy: Around the same time, Alternate ROOTS, a community-based arts organization committed to social justice in the South, was encouraging ArtSpot to host a regional gathering. In the lead up, we talked a lot about how the black/white racial dynamic in the region tended to dominate our conversations, and how we needed to step outside of that polarity and work with other artists. We especially needed to learn from indigenous American artists.

In late June of 2006, we co-hosted "State of the Nation III: Restoration" at Ashé Cultural Arts Center in New Orleans. In the wake of Katrina, my long-time partner, Sean LaRocca, and I were married and pregnant by Halloween. My insomnial pregnancy hormones, toxic refrigerator mold fumes, and some assistance from the divine muse inspired a new performance piece for the gathering at Ashé. All it needed was a cane and the costume I'd worn in our last piece pre-Katrina: a long sparkly purple evening gown

Geodesic Dome | Bayou Terre-aux-Boeufs | 2006
Chief Albert Naquin of the Isle de Jean Charles Band of Chitimatcha, Choctaw, Biloxi Confederation of Muskogees, told us that Pacific Domes Northwest wanted to donate 16-foot geodesic domes to tribal citizens to help people get back home. We accepted one for our homestead in St. Bernard. At first, we set it up as a symbol that we were coming home. Later, it was used as retreat from the sun, a greenhouse, a studio space, a frame to grow maypop, and a shelter for my dog, Queenie. Photograph by Mark Krasnoff.

with a low neckline and high slits up my thighs that were stretched by my third trimester belly. To me, the spirit of "Momma Nola" was a 288-year-old Storyville brothel madam who was tough as nails, beautiful, rotten and fresh off of life support. A mother to many—her own and her adopted children—she loves them all, she takes them all in, and she requires them all to give something back to keep it all going. Momma Nola talks trash with the audience. Some people talk back and some people are too afraid to be called forth during a performance. In the dark, I heard someone call "Hey, Momma Nola!" I recognized his voice. It was Krasnoff. She answered him back, "Hey baby…Hey my baby! How you doin'?

Krasnoff: Oooooooh, it's rough out here, Momma.

Momma Nola: Yeah, I know baby, I know, sweetie. But you made it. You're still here. It's sooooooo good to hear your voice.

Monique with Gas Mask | **St. Bernard Parish** | **2006**
Post-Katrina, Krasnoff and I had been warned about the toxic conditions found in the flooded areas surrounding the "Isle of Denial." Naively, we invested in a respirator masks thinking it would help to protect our health, which eventually became this symbolic object we integrated into the documentation. This image was taken by Krasnoff at the intersection of Paris Road and St. Bernard Highway. On the other side of the spray painted signs are the St. Bernard Parish prison and one of Louisiana's oldest refineries.

Krasnoff: You too, Momma Nola, you lookin' fine!

Momma Nola: Now you know you're a liar. But thank you baby. Momma loves you.

Krasnoff: I love you too, Momma, we're tryin' to keep you here, so hang in there.

At the end of the night, we returned to ourselves, and Krasnoff introduced me to a young woman; pretty with long dark hair. It was Monique. He said they were working on a film and they'd like to share it the next night. And we did. It was the beginning of their film, *My Louisiana Love*, and we were all blown away: "Oh my God, an indigenous Louisiana artist opening a window into what was going on in the indigenous communities along the coast. Finally. Hallelujah! We should all just shut up now. I should shut up now." Monique and Krasnoff were capturing everything. Wherever the next problem was, they were there with the camera. They were filming every moment of their lives with their face masks and hazmat suits.

Monique: I was a wreck from losing my dad, and Krasnoff had become manic. He started with one antidepressant and then changed to another. In his younger days in Australia, he took a bunch of pills and tried to commit suicide by swimming out into the ocean. Like global warming, the story seemed far away. Of the two of us, I thought of him as the strong one.

One morning in September, I woke up in a fright—unable to breathe. I turned to Krasnoff in bed next to me, and thought it was just a bad dream. That evening, I came home from work to find all of his affairs laid out on the floor of our living room with a suicide letter left behind. He had stayed up all night writing his final words before coming back to bed with me before his last sunrise. He wrote to me:

Do your work Verdin, the world needs you in it for there to be hope, beauty and goodness, for this is what you are. I've said it a thousand times.

My love for you is eternal! I am sorry, Mo, that I hurt you in this way. I could not bear anymore what was happening to me, inside of me. My own circumstances and disease were my own. If anything, you gave me hope and enlightenment in theses times where I could not see any. Our journey and work together is one of the pinnacles of my life.

Without you, all of this greatness which we captured could not and would not be possible to have the future it merits and shares. Mostly, it is your vision of love and beauty which is the standard of how I hope all things come to pass for the rest of the earth. Take the work, your work and spread it to the world. It is of the utmost in importance and a necessity for healing humanity!

After I left the house, he walked down to the Mississippi River to take his own life.

Kathy: He did it at the Fly. He went there, and he shot himself. I knew it had been rough for him— it was rough for all of us—but I had no idea it had been that rough. And he was putting the roughness out there. He had never shied away from it. When did rough become unbearable? And Monique was his lover. How did she cope? What did his family think? How do you ask? How do you talk about it? I went to Krasnoff's memorial second line to celebrate his life—his wildness, his beauty, his insistence on art and truth, his loup garou.

The Loup Garou's Boat | **New Orleans** | **2009**
Photograph by Libby Nevinger, courtesy of ArtSpot Productions and Mondo Bizarro.

HERE I AM!
by blood and spit
by dirt and bone
I'm telling y'all hungry ghosts
leave me alone!

Lord, wash me of my inequities
cleanse me of my sins

—Raymond "Moose" Jackson,
The Loup Garou: A Lunar Cycle

Bernard Williams with "Ghost Trails" | **Mississippi River** | **2011**

In 2011, I was at A Studio in the Woods, an artist residency on the Westbank of New Orleans, to work on the film Krasnoff and I began together, which became *My Louisiana Love.* At the same time, the sculptor Bernard Williams was working on a sculpture based on the drawings by Howard Fisk in the 1940s of the ancient paths of the Mississippi River. The cartography was drawn for the Army Corps of Engineers but is also an incredible collection of art.

Bernard Williams wrote of his time at A Studio in the Woods: "Early on during my stay, I was taken with newspaper reports of a young man losing his life in the river. This became a subtext for my sculpture project concerned with invisible root systems and the river's meandering history. I decided to mount the river myself, to risk the river. Getting onto the river with the sculpture and the raft became a sort of meditation on all the mentioned aspects of the river: the invisible undercurrents, early riverboat traffic among flatboats, keelboats, and steamboats delivering cargo of all types, the fantastic meandering routes, and the river's appetite for consumption."

and the Pointe a la Hache ferryman

waved a beatific goodbye

WARNING
NATURAL GAS
PIPELINE CROSSING
TEXACO PIPELINES LLC
1-800-762-2404

as it all turned into grass and oilpits

sinking into the sea

"Finistere Louisiane 6"
Raymond "Moose" Jackson's poem collage with one of my photographs.

A Trilogy

Monique: There is something about synchronicity in New Orleans, slightly off, but right on time. Unexpected moments can change the course of one's life in a second. After Krasnoff died, I was walking Queenie and a friend's dog in the Lower Garden District, when the three of us almost collided with a man with a Mohawk on a red Schwinn bicycle. It was curious moment that lasted a few seconds but lingered with a, "What is that about?"

A few days later, I was reading the St. Bernard newspaper at Matine's kitchen table and saw a photo of Nunez Community College faculty, which included the director of the

theater program, Nick Slie. It was the same guy Queenie had almost knocked off his bicycle. I was compelled to write a letter of introduction to him.

Nick Slie, Co-Artistic Director of Mondo Bizarro: A couple days later, there was a note on my car at Nunez Community College. It was tucked into to one of Monique's incredible photographs and said that I should come "down the road" some day to see her family's home and land. It wasn't long until I found myself moving through 200-year-old oak trees, swatting mosquitoes, in the woods behind Matine's house.

Loup Garou | **City Park, New Orleans** | **2009**
Nick Slie as the werewolf, Loup Garou, in the abandoned golf courses in City Park. Behind him are waves: "*j'ai dit adieu à le mer, ma mére.* (i have said goodbye to the sea, my mother.)" Photograph by Libby Nevinger, courtesy of ArtSpot Productions and Mondo Bizarro.

Monique: I invited Nick to an installation down in Pointe-aux-Chenes. During the annual boat blessing, I planned to set up a geodesic dome that had been donated to my family as an exhibit and distribute family photos in Anesie and Jane's front yard. Nick couldn't make it, but the founders of A Studio in the Woods, Joe and Lucianne Carmichael, pulled up in their minivan. Out popped Raymond "Moose" Jackson, a tall man with suspenders on. Matine said, "He must not be from around here. Too tall. He must be from somewhere up north." He was a poet. At the end of the day, the Carmichaels left him with us to help deinstall the dome, and on our way back to the city, we stopped at Bisland Cemetery to watch the sunset.

Raymond "Moose" Jackson: I was born in Detroit and watched how Michigan had been destroyed by industry. My family is part Shawnee and Cherokee from Kentucky. After leaving the military, I ended up in New Orleans via train hopping, hitchhiking, and direct action. My work had

been focusing on the environmental impact of industry on the fragile wetlands of Louisiana. Here was the front line. Along the bayou, Monique's family was boiling crawfish and shrimp, and the fleet was getting blessed by a priest. These folks were native, they spoke French, and their neighbors were Mexican and black Creoles.

Monique: Moose and I began to take drives to the ends of the roads in south Louisiana just to see what was there. He scratched notes in his journal, and at the end of the day, he looked up and said, "I think I just found a new friend," before reciting slices of our drive woven with threads of history. In 2009, our worlds became more intertwined when he wrote the environmental poem-play, *Loup Garou,* and Nick took on the role for the solo performance co-produced by Kathy's theater company. In one of her introductions to the play, she wrote:

Hanging Landscapes | **City Park, New Orleans** | **2009**
My photographs of Pointe-aux-Chenes and St. Bernard Parish on display as part of *Loup Garou* in City Park.

Loup Garou began one full moon midnight in 2007, with a howl and a pact over a pint of Abita with Nick Slie...Or did it begin the night I heard Mark Krasnoff shot himself at the Fly? Or the last time my brother-in-law went off the wagon for Mardi Gras? Or with my first fear of dogs? The DivineWolf called out to each collaborator and asked us to listen.

Nick: In those holy days of 2009, we still could not fathom how long it would take to sift through the ruins left by Katrina, nor could any of us have predicted how much change was yet to come. But we had one another, suspended in a web of uncertainty, trusting the known and unknown forces that brought us together. As Moose would write years later, "It was more important to be family, to be together, than to have someplace to live."

When we were working on *Loup Garou*, we all had a sense that this work was coming from a source that was good and true, dancing that fine line between wanting the artistic product to be clear while surrendering to the greater forces—known and unknown—that seemed to be guiding us. The creative team was from many different places, with varied connections to Southeast Louisiana; however, the listening was deep, especially when it came to Moose's writing.

Moose: Nick played the role of Sebastian Couteau. His last name means "knife" in French, and is also a family name of one of Monique's ancestors. In the Cajun legends, the curse of the loup garou is usually an affliction caused by some anguish—often a love affair gone wrong—but it could be a family curse. It happened to people who got too far out in the swamp and bonded more to the land than to

Against the Chemical Plants | **St. James Parish** | **2019**
Today, St. James Parish is in the heart of "Cancer Alley," saturated with petrochemical facilities—a part of the strategic oil reserve and a kind of terminal for crude. It is the end point for the Bayou Bridge Pipeline, which connects with the Dakota Access Pipeline, and carries Bakken shale across the United States. Following the Mississippi watershed, it risks crossing the Atchafalaya Basin, America's largest swamp, to tie into another pipeline to ship material further south to be refined, or to transport for international export.

their community. Sebastian suffered on all those accounts. He also suffers from amnesia and in the play, he tries to piece his story together, recalling what the Cajuns suffered and what is happening to the land. The play took place at dawn and dusk in the abandoned, re-wilding parts of City Park in New Orleans.

Kathy: Monique put up an outdoor gallery of her family photos for folks to look at on the way to the performance.

Nick: I remember drinking coffee on the back of a truck as Monique stretched old green fishing net across the land to determine the best way to suspend some incredible maps

and photos of Southeast Louisiana across old oaks. I'm not sure how this all ever came to be. It was less planned than needed, less a project than a necessity.

Years later, after my grandmother Rita passed, I inherited the names of our ancestors in St. James Parish all the way back to 1719. My first written ancestor? Sebastian Loup. A couple years after that, Monique begins to search deeper into her own family records and discovers that many of her ancestors lived in and around St. James Parish. Turns out the family bonds were even closer than I thought.

Moose: The knife is real.

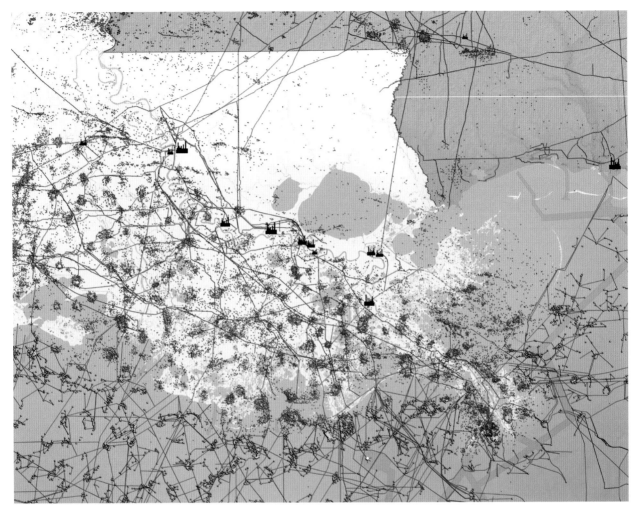

Network of oil pipelines off and on shore in Louisiana. Map from Anthony Fontenot and Jakob Rosenzweig's *Exposing New Orleans* project.

My eyes are hot
tired of vision
tired of seeing our doom
Ten years from now
this land is gone
our people a memory
our way of life
disappeared

Twenty years from now
the yoke of industry
virtual reality
prison economy
has this country on its knees

I would not want to be here
when the beast you created
breaks its fetters and is free

–Raymond "Moose" Jackson,
The Loup Garou: A Lunar Cycle

Cry You One: A New Cypress Tree | **40 Arpent Canal, St. Bernard Parish** | **2013**
At the end of *Cry You One*, Peter J. Bowling and I paddled a small Louisiana bald cypress tree into the swamp. Photograph by Melisa Cardona, courtesy of ArtSpot Productions and Mondo Bizarro.

Kathy: After we finished the production of *Loup Garou*, Nick dreamed *Cry You One*.

Monique: It was a procession/performance/eco-experience about land loss in South Louisiana.

Kathy: He wanted to do it in St. Bernard, where Nunez Community College is located. And if we were going to do anything in St. Bernard, we had to work with Monique. In 2012, we asked her to be on the visual artist team.

Monique: The goal was to take an audience on a mile and a half walk along a man-made, earthen levee built in St. Bernard Parish to keep surge waters out. During my father's childhood, the area was a cypress swamp so thick you could not see the sun, but now, like down in Pointe-aux-Chenes, the trees were mostly skeletons. The

Mississippi River Gulf Outlet, which has been responsible for so much of the flood damage from Katrina, also sucked saltwater deep into what was once a fresh and brackish ecosystem, singeing the cypress forest and live oak tree ridges. It was hard not to be despondent, but *Cry You One* ended at a pumping station where a baby cypress forest was growing due to freshwater being pumped out of nearby neighborhoods.

Kathy: In the early days of the rehearsal process, everybody was doing all of the assignments—visual, movement, song. We participated in all the art forms that we were trying to blend together.

Monique: I watched my friends transform into characters, who embodied information and story, and blended the lines between truth and imagination.

Cry You One: Inside My Eminent Domain | **40 Arpent Canal, St. Bernard Parish** | **2013**
In the geodesic dome, I wove transparent images of my photographs of my family into the shrimp netting covered with an amber mesh. The sun shone through the palmettos to illuminate the images from the outside. Photograph by Melisa Cardona, courtesy of ArtSpot Productions and Mondo Bizrro.

Kathy: I kept looking at Monique. She is, was, will always be so beautiful—comfortable in her skin and open. I asked her if she would perform, and she became our protagonist, surrounded by a motley crew of environmentalists, scientists, ethnomusicologists, boars, snakes, alligators, spiders, coyotes, and hawks. She played herself— an indigenous Louisiana woman with deep roots to this place, committed to its survival, and if not that, then to telling the tale of what happened here.

Monique: Moose wrote poems inspired by south Louisiana that I recited for the play. Jeff Becker, the lead designer of the show, built a small boat to ferry our audience across the 40 Arpent drainage canal from the real world to the dream world we created along the levee, but it only held 15 people and our audiences were often more than 60. We needed a place for people to wait until it was their turn to cross. We decided to cover my geode-

sic dome with palmettos to make it look like a traditional Houma structure.

As our audience approached during the performances, I hid inside the dome and popped out of the roof—as though the structure was a gigantic skirt—and then welcomed our guests to my eminent domain. I was occupying this space because the "risk reducers" were threatening to mine the land beneath my feet to build earthen levees. Inside the hut, I told stories of my family. As they left, I gave each group a button bush seed, and explained, "This is medicine for the land."

Button bush is a native tree traditionally known to be medicinal. Native tribes used the bark to make washes that were good skin astringents, and teas that helped with inflammation, headaches, fever, and venereal diseases. The bark was also chewed to relieve toothaches. Roots could

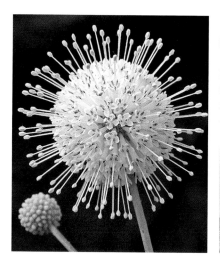 

Left: A button bush flower, by Bob Peterson. ***Right:*** Back home on Bayou Terre-aux-Beoufs with Matine in 2012. Photograph by Marie Baronnet.

be used for muscle inflammation and to support the blood. Button bush is good for restoring wetlands, too. It likes to live in the riparian zone, and is well loved by ducks and other water birds for food and a resting spots. Its roots can slow and combat erosion. The groups carried the seeds with them on the mile journey down the levee, and tossed them out into St. Bernard Parish's Central Wetlands at the end of the show.

I had only five minutes with each group, but getting people under the same roof to sit in a circle and witness a little piece of south Louisiana truth was powerful. I was inspired to create spaces to continue conversations about our relationship to the environment and its climate; to consider our cultural vulnerabilities, possibilities, and traditional remedies. The palmetto hut was transportable through time and physical locations. It connected me back to Matine's early childhood, the photographs she showed me when I was young. It connected me to my own. When I was a little girl, upset and a little heartbroken by disappointment, Matine calmly took me outside to help plant flowers in her garden, and distracted my tears by keeping my hands in the dirt. When I was ten years old, she planted cypress trees in the front yard by the bayouside. They now tower 60 feet tall, glowing burnt rust orange in the winter, before they go bald in the winter.

Recoveries

On Thanksgiving Day 2013, Matine fell. She was 98 years old. Everyone kept saying, "Oh, you know how it is. Old people break their hip and then they don't live much longer." Not only did she break her hip, she also broke her wrist, which complicated the road to recovery and the use of a walker. While in the hospital, she didn't want to drink water because it was from the tap. She could tell if water was from the rain or from the river almost as quickly as she could taste if shrimp were caught offshore or from the bayous of the marsh. She refused to eat offshore shrimp, because she didn't like the taste of the iodine, and only used treated river water from the tap as a last resort. I started bringing gallons of rain water to the hospital. She got back up and kept moving. Within six weeks time, she was back home, but in need of full-time assistance.

I am incredibly grateful for the 36 years we had together, but I'm especially grateful to have been with her during the sunset of her life. Sometimes she would remind me, "I took care of you when you were little, now it's your turn to take care of me, *Cheré*." Not in a "you owe me" kind of way, but, "Life is like a circle. We have been here before." And then she would apologize for being a burden, irritated that her body was breaking down—that she couldn't do for herself.

For her last seasons, I re-prioritized to be home with her and Uncle Xavier. I worked part-time so that I could take care of them on our land. I planted our garden, and learned how to cook biscuits, gumbo, beans, etouffee, and fricassee Matine's way. When she was well enough, and if she was interested, I took her to screenings and other social engagements to get out the house. The Land Memory Bank and Seed Exchange project, a collective of artists, historians, architects, scientists, and delta lovers, was incubated during this time.

We moved Xavier into a nursing home on the Westbank close to one of my aunts. I knew it was his worst nightmare, but he was never one to complain. We missed his quiet presence. A year later, Matine and I made our last drive to Terrebonne Parish with Vivian and my best friend, Sharon Linezo Hong, to prepare my grandfather and great-grandmother's graves for the All Saints' Day celebrations. The second most intense tropical cyclone ever recorded, Hurricane Patricia, had crashed into Central America and crossed into the Gulf of Mexico. Remnants of her wrath were beginning to push in a wake of gray skies and rising tides. The further down the bayou we went, the more the old ladies kept saying "*Bon Dieu!* Look how high the water is! And it just keeps coming up."

Sharon and I convinced the old ladies to take a long detour down to Bayou Grand Calliou to see one of the biggest Indian mounds in the Delta and then cut through the marsh to Bayou Petite Calliou near Cocodrie to visit the Picou Cemetery, where Touh-la-bay Courteau, our Biloxi Medal Chief ancestor, is said to have owned land and been buried. The site is an ancient Indian mound dating from 1000 AD. When we finally got to Bisland Cemetery, the sky started to spit rain. I knew this was the place that Matine really wanted to be. When she died on April 18, 2016—ten days past her 101st birthday—we kept all of her funeral wishes, down to the very last one: that witnesses stay behind and make sure the concrete top was set back in place on the tomb after her body was lowered in to join Toussaint's.

It was hard to go back to St. Bernard after Matine was gone. I had never known the land without her. Everything reminded me of her. I moved up the road to Arabi, the

Matine's Burial | **Bayou Terrebonne** | **2016**

"Garden District" of St. Bernard Parish, just on the south of where my mom and I lived in the Lower Ninth Ward when I was a young girl. I was grateful for the space, but it never felt like home. I couldn't get used to that sour-sweet smell coming from the Domino Sugar Refinery and petrochemical plants. I missed the rhythms we developed around our garden, the sound of owls at night.

Return to the Water

Over the years, Nick has invited me back to Nunez Community College to talk to his students about *My Louisiana Love*. When I talk to them about what is happening with land loss, it surprises me how little they know about the environment that surrounds them. Many of them are born and raised in St. Bernard and lived through Hurricane Katrina as little kids, but do not know why south Louisiana is disappearing, or what is being done to try to prevent more erosion.

The state of Louisiana has a 50 billion dollar, 50-year plan called the Coastal Master Plan. Funding is heavily dependent upon the state receiving deep water oil and gas royal-

Medicine Wheel Garden | **St. Bernard Parish** | **2017**
Here I am at the annual Los Isleños Fiesta with Tammy Greer, a United Houma Nation tribal member and the director of the Center for American Indian Research and Studies (CAIRS) at the University of Southern Mississippi. She is talking with me about plants at the Medicine Wheel Garden, part of the Land Memory Bank and Seed Exchange Project. Behind us is the traditional palmetto structure built for the project as well. Since 2005, Dr. Greer has been stewarding a medicine wheel garden at her university and brought starts from the big garden on her campus. Photograph by Sabree Hill.

ties coming from the Gulf of Mexico. The hope is that fossil fuel production will grow exponentially into the infinite future off the coast of Louisiana to generate income that can be allocated to coastal restoration efforts. The way the plan is currently set up, the restoration of the coast of south Louisiana will be brought to you by the extraction of carbon, at an exponential rate, into the unforeseen future. The only reason we currently have significant dollars to put toward restoration projects is because of the fines BP (British Petroleum) was forced to pay after the 2010 Deepwater Horizon oil spill included allocations such as barrier island restoration, sediment river diversions, and the building of living shorelines.

These projects, along with flood protection, bring mixed results. During the summer of 2017, loads of dirt were mined from coastal properties to levee lower Pointe-aux-Chenes inside the "Morganza to the Gulf" system with a floodgate installed on the bayou near the end of the road. But water follows the paths of least resistance. Storm surges now push the sea further inland to flood communities that historically didn't, which creates new vulnerabilities. Left out of the levee system in Terrebonne Parish, in 2016, Isle de Jean Charles was awarded the first climate relocation grant by the federal government, which has set a precedent in the state that the only option for coastal communities is to retreat.

Floating Lab | **Bayou Pointe-aux-Chenes** | **2019**

In Terrebonne Parish, many of my cousins are welders who have worked in the oil field and at sugar mills while still carrying on the tradition of boatbuilding. Our ancestors carved flat bottomed pirogue boats out of ancient cypress; now they have mastered the building of Lafitte Skiffs, a flat-bottomed fishing boat. In the spring of 2019, I worked with the Delta Collective and Another Gulf is Possible to commission my cousin Anesie "T'Dun" Verdin, Jr., and his son, Justin, to weld us a floating platform. We plan to use it as a Float Lab to begin testing solutions for migration adaptations. We imagine the floating lab as a transformative space that can move from bayou to bayou to be used as a food sovereignty resource as well as an exhibition and data collection site.

As I think about these decisions, I come back to an exercise that Nick gives his students. He asks them to write their own obituaries, but he doesn't call it that—he frames it more as, "When you die, what do you want to be written about your life?" Since I was 18, I've said I want really simple things in life: to be in good company in beautiful places, eating good food. To be, for instance, with a flock of ibis feeding in my front yard. Like the ibis, we may have to pick up and move, and then come back home, returning to the cyclical migrations of our ancestors.

TIMELINE OF IMAGERY

Now Open in Venice | **Los Angeles, California** | **2005**
After Katrina, Krasnoff and I collected yard signs we found on neutral grounds across the city. We shipped a big box of our collection out to California and stuck them in the yard outside of the Social and Public Art Resource Center for the opening of my first official exhibition, *Sauvage Mélange* (Wild Mix).

Fall 2005. Mike Davis, the apocalyptic urban theorist who wrote *Ecology of Fear*, came to New Orleans, and asked Krasnoff what he could do to help. Krasnoff gave him a CD of my photographs of Grand Bois and Pointe-aux-Chenes. Within a few weeks, Mike and his wife, Alessandra Moctezuma, the director of San Diego's Mesa College Art Gallery, set up two exhibitions of my photographs, as well as a speaking tour at University of California campuses in the southern part of the state. I went out to California for a month, and had my first gallery showing in Venice, Los Angeles, at the Social Public Art Resource Center.

June 15, 2006. In southwest Louisiana, the town of Arnaudville was built at an Atakapa-Ishak trading post at the intersection of Bayou Teche and the Bayou Fuselier. Krasnoff and I fell in love with the creative place-making

happening there as we witnessed how the development of Nunu's Collective helped to revitalize the country town. I was invited to exhibit my work in a little Creole cabin alongside Bayou Fuselier. It opened the day after my dad passed away. I was feeling sad and uncomfortable throughout my artist's talk, and then a woman in the audience started screaming. Her hair had caught on fire and the whole gallery was full of the smoke. My reaction, "Abandon awkwardness! This woman is on fire!" was a metaphor for what was going on with climate change in general and helped me gain confidence to show my work.

August 2006. A rough cut of *My Louisiana Love* was screened at Alternative ROOTS' "State of the Nation III: Restoration" at Ashé Cultural Arts Center in New Orleans.

Left: Kathy Randels performing in *Beneath the Strata/Disappearing*. Photograph by Libby Nevinger, courtesy of ArtSpot Productions. *Middle:* Nick Slie as the Loup Garou. Photograph by Libby Nevinger, courtesy of ArtSpot Productions and Mondo Bizarro. *Right:* A photograph I took of Raymond "Moose" Jackson reading his poetry.

September 2006. Mark Krasnoff's funeral. Richard Valadie, mastermind of carnival and beloved friend of Krasnoff's, built a shopping cart float with a cut-out of Kras on top that we wheeled through the streets of the old Quarters to the Mississippi River. The Soul Rebels Brass Band serenaded the procession as we carried a pile of palmetto ashes Krasnoff had burned on Ash Wednesday. The second line ended at Café Brasil.

January 2007. Opening of "Louisiana Left Behind" at Georgia College & State University in Milledgeville, Georgia. The small town is located on conquistador Hernando de Soto's march through the region in 1540. It was the capital of Georgia during the Civil War, and the site of the state's largest mental institution. I exhibited the series "Coffin Boxes." Viewers were encouraged to open the boxes mounted on the walls to see inside.

May 2007. At the end of my artist talk at Georgia College, a professor handed me an application for A Studio in the Woods' "Restoration Residency." My proposal was simple—to have time to stop to sift through the 65 hours of film footage Krasnoff and I gathered before he died so that the documentary could move forward. The artist retreat on eight acres of forest next to the Mississippi River was

started by a couple, Joe and Lucianne Carmichael, and their network of friends who were artists, ecologists, and educators. Lucianne had been the principal of McDonogh 15, an arts-based public elementary school in New Orleans, for many years. Like my grandparents, they had built their own home on the land. It is both a beautiful retreat and a space committed to protecting the environment of south Louisiana.

I invited my best friend, Sharon Linezo Hong, out to the woods to help me make sense of what Krasnoff and I had been doing. We called the tapes "the Baby." Total novice filmmakers, Sharon helped me look deeply at all the layers of the stories, and we began to incorporate my photographs throughout the documentary as well. There were many times when we both wanted to give up out of frustration, but then one of us would rally. I remember Sharon telling me, "We can't let the story sink in the swamp." I would be lost without her.

Spring 2008. With the help of Sharon and carnival float builder/engineer Casey Valadie, I set-up the pop-up gallery (with the geodesic dome covered in fishing nets) in Jane and Anesie's front yard in Pointe-aux-Chenes during the annual Blessing of the Boats.

Fall 2008. Ken Wells invited me to contribute photographs for *The Good Pirates of the Forgotten Bayous: Fighting to Save a Way of Life in the Wake of Katrina*, published by Yale University Press. It includes a chapter with Matine, Xavier, and my dad's Katrina survival stories.

August 2009. A classic sweaty Louisiana summer night. As the city arts scene celebrated its annual White Linen Night, the Three Ring Circus in Central City hosted an exhibit for Wet Linen Night. In preparation, ultimate junker and sculptor, Adam Tourek, collected hoses from garbage piles and built a rain machine that we hung from the side of the building. Inside the gallery, I installed an exhibit "A Decade of Reflection," which included the coffin boxes and the black and white photographs strung along a clothesline. As a tease for what was to come, the *Loup Garou* showed up for a street performance. A Cajun band started to play and the gallery turned into a dance hall.

Fall 2009. *Loup Garou* debuted at City Park in New Orleans, and I incorporated shrimp nets into the outdoor installation of my photographs.

Summer 2010. A collection of my photographs from the Louisiana wetlands was used in the research project, "Mississippi Delta: Constructing with Water," for the United States' Pavilion for the Twelfth International Architecture Exhibition for La Biennale Di Venezia in Italy. The work is published in the U.S. Pavilion catalog, *Workbook*, published by Princeton Architectural Press in 2010.

Fall 2011. Opening of "Disappearing Landscapes: The American Delta in Distress" at Mesa College in San Diego, California. The exhibit shared photographs of my Houma family and cartographic data maps produced by Anthony Fontenot and Jakob Rozensweig investigating the complex relationships between the geological, infrastructural, and ecological layers in the Delta region.

Top: Matine and Xavier came to the opening of "A Decade of Reflection" at the Three Ring Circus. Photograph by Joe Denmon. **Bottom:** Talking with an audience at *Cry You One* from the top of the geodesic dome transformed into a palmetto hut. Photograph by Melisa Cardona.

Summer 2012. *My Louisiana Love* premiered at the Smithsonian's National Museum of the American Indian. The film went on to win Best Documentary at Toronto's 2012 imagineNATIVE Film and Media Arts Festival, and was shown on public television in the United States and Australia.

2013. I contributed a chapter, "Ebb & Flow: Southward into Vanishing Lands," to *Unfathomable City: A New Orleans Atlas*, edited by Rebecca Solnit & Rebecca Snedeker and published by the University of California Press.

2013. Premiere of *Cry You One* in the wetlands of eastern St. Bernard Parish before we took the show on the road

Anesie, Julio, & Me
Historic New Orleans Collection | 2017

for a national tour, which included 10' x 5' reproductions of my photographs from Terrebonne and St. Bernard Parishes.

2015. The Land Memory Bank and Seed Exchange was funded by Platforms, which supports self-organized artistic projects in and around New Orleans through funding from the Andy Warhol Foundation regranted by local organizations Antenna, Ashé, and (at that time) Pelican Bomb. We began the Land Memory Bank at the Los Isleños Museum in St. Bernard Parish, using the geodesic dome to build a palmetto hut and adding a couple of lean-tos.

August 2015. The Land Memory Bank was relocated to Crevasse-22, an art space owned by Sidney Torres III and developed by Jeanne Nathan and the Creative Alliance of New Orleans for a show called "The Spirit of the People of St. Bernard." Up the road from Matine's land, the site is on the former Poydras Plantation, named after the French colonist Julien Poydras. Born in Brittany in 1740, Poydras joined the French navy and was captured by the

British and brought to London when he was 20 years old. In the 1760s, he escaped on a boat headed to the sugar colony of Saint-Domingue and then relocated to Louisiana where he bought plantations in Pointe Coupee Parish and St. Bernard. It is here that Bayou Terre-aux-Boeufs once branched from the Mississippi River. In the spring of 1922, a natural crevasse flooded the parish. Despite the floods of 1922 and 1927, and the installation of Louisiana's premier freshwater diversion project just a few miles away, the area still maintains part of St. Bernard's natural beauty, and the art show attracted thousands of visitors.

September 2015. On a hot summer day, Matine and Vivian crammed into my Prius with a wheelchair and a bunch of art to help me install an exhibit inside the Los Isleños' Ducros Museum, "Honoring our Ancestors." They ate shrimp po-boys from Guillory's Green Store and took little naps as I climbed up and down a ladder to hang photographs. When they woke up, I told them I was not completely satisfied with the resolution of the images, and wished the hardware for the framing had been better. Matine shook her head and said, "Monique, your eyes are too good."

December 2015. I brought *My Louisiana Love* to France to share in the countryside of Ardeche as well as in and around Paris during the 21st Annual International Climate Conference of Parties (COP21). Through the Indigenous Environmental Network, I connected with people from the Amazon to Alaska, as well as other parts of the world. We shared stories of how our communities have endured corporate colonial practices and the side effects of fossil fuel extraction.

Spring 2016. At the Isleño Museum's Fiesta, coastal conservationist Blaise Pezold (who had experience building palmetto structures with my cousin Pete Billiot) and I constructed a traditional palmetto hut about 16 feet in diameter with Donny Verdin, Tammy Greer, and their families. The next year, when we tore down the old structure, Tammy said, "Well, now that's a perfect place to plant a medicine wheel garden." A professor at University of Southern Mississippi, she has one on her campus. We like to think of our medicine garden in St. Bernard as its offspring. It has become an intertribal, multicultural, and intergenerational magnet.

May 2016. The Shell Annual General meeting at the Hague, Netherlands, allies helped me hold up my photographs used in *Cry You One* to reflect realities of life in Louisiana.

Spring 2017. The Bayou Bridge Pipeline resistance camp, L'eau Est La Vie, opened. Friends from the Indigenous Environmental Network came to my family land in St. Bernard to harvest palmettos to build shelter at the camp. We went into the bottom lands where the 100-year palmetto groves grow under ancient oaks to sustainably harvest fronds that would provide shade.

Spring of 2017. A Studio in the Woods invited me to pilot its "Adaptations" residency program.

November 2017. Curator of Prospect.4: The Lotus in Spite of the Swamp, Trevor Schoonmaker, invited me to exhibit my black-and-white photographs at The Historic New Orleans Collection's Laura Simon Nelson Galleries. I wove dried palmettos to create window tapestries to hang in the windows of their old storefront gallery.

During the exhibit, I spoke to the HNOC's docents about the work. At the end of the presentation, an older woman told me she was born in the city of Houma in the 1920s. She remembered it as a sugar town before the oil and gas boom hit, and pointed out that the family who endowed the HNOC—the Williams family—were the owners of the F. B. Williams Cypress Company. In the early 20th century, the company dredged canals through thousands of acres of swampland to log cypress trees until the wetlands were almost completely deforested. The company then turned their investments towards the oil and gas industry. While trying not to look like I just got hit over the head by a 2x4, I managed to say, "Oh, really!?"

"Oh really, not surprising!" would have been a better response. Most arts and culture in south Louisiana are brought to you by name-your-oil-and-or-gas-company: The New Orleans Jazz and Heritage Festival brought to you by Shell Oil; French Quarter Festival brought to you by Chevron; open museum days for locals at The New Orleans Museum of Art, Contemporary Arts Center, and the Ogden Museum of Southern Art brought to you by the Helis Foundation. Energy companies in Louisiana support the spectrum ranging from science, technology, engineering and math projects in public schools to food pantries, festivals, and scholarships.

December 2017. I joined the Another Gulf is Possible collective as part of the core leadership circle of brown (Desi, Latinx and Indigenous) women from Brownsville, Texas to Pensacola, Florida, to build pathways for just transitions around land loss and climate change.

Julio and Monique
2018 | Gran Canaria
Talking with Julio Blancas on the island of Gran Canaria. Its city, the port of Las Palmas, was the last stop for Christopher Columbus, and all the conquistadors that followed him into the Atlantic Ocean.

2018. I was the inaugural Rosenthal-Blumenfeld Gulf South Foodways Fellow at the New Orleans Center for the Gulf South at Tulane University.

April 2018. I co-curated Fossil Free Festival, a weeklong festival of art, food, music, film screenings, and workshops focused on the ethics and complexities of funding art and education with fossil fuel money and imagining a Fossil Free Culture.

October–December 2018. In honor of the tricentennial of New Orleans, the Cultural Office of the Embassy of Spain and Spain-USA Foundation envisioned a cultural exchange between New Orleans and Las Palmas, Canary Islands—the original home of the Isleños. A Studio in the Woods facilitated the call-out, and I was selected for a residency at La Regenta, an art center in Las Palmas, where I met the artist Julio Blancas before he came to A Studio in the Woods.

August 29, 2019. With support from Another Gulf is Possible, the Delta Collective (Anthony Fontenot, Jakob Rozensweig, and myself) curated "Floating Cities." It opened on the 14th anniversary of Hurricane Katrina at the Zeitgeist Multidisciplinary Arts Center in Arabi, Louisiana.

Fall 2019. I was invited by the University of Minnesota's Itasca Biological Field Station, the Weisman Art Museum, and A Studio in the Woods to pilot "Big River Continuum" exchange between the headwaters and the Mississippi River delta.

WORKS CONSULTED

Look Out | **2005** | **Grand Bois**
Leo Rodriguez in a boat being built in a shipyard in Grand Bois.

Abruzzo, Emily. 2010. *Workbook: The Official Catalog for Workshopping: An American Model for Architectural Practice*. Princeton: Princeton University Press.

Becnel, Thomas A. 1996. *Senator Allen Ellender of Louisiana: A Biography*. Baton Rouge: Louisiana State University Press.

Bourgeois, Lillian C. 1957. *Cabanocey: The History, Customs, and Folklore of St. James Parish*. New Orleans: Pelican Publishing Company.

Campbell, Marie McDowell Pilkington. 1981. *Nostalgic Notes on St. James Parish, Louisiana: Then and Now*. Edited by Lee Etheredge Patrick. Baton Rouge: Self-Published.

Dardar, T. Mayheart. 2014. *Istrouma: A Houma Manifesto*. Shreveport: Centenary College of Louisiana Press (Cahiers du Tintamorre).

Davis, Mike. 1999. *Ecology of Fear: Los Angeles and the Imaginiation of Disaster*. New York: Vintage.

DeSantis, John. 2016. *The Thibodaux Massacre: Racial Violence and the 1887 Sugar Cane Labor Strike*. Charleston, South Carolina: The History Press.

Dier, Chris. 2017. *The 1868 St. Bernard Parish Massacre: Blood in the Cane Fields*. Charleston, South Carolina: The History Press.

Darensbourg, Jeffery, Ed. 2018. *Bulbancha is Still A Place*. New Orleans: POC Zine Project.

Ethridge, Robbie. 2009. "Introduction" in *Mapping the Mississippian Shatter Zone: The Colonial Indian Trade and Regional Instability in the American South*. Edited by Robbie Ethridge and Sheri M. Shuck-Hall. Lincoln: University of Nebraska Press.

Gallay, Alan. 2002. *The Indian Slave Trade: The Rise of the English Empire in the American South, 1670-1717*. New Haven, CT: Yale University Press.

Gowland, Bryan, M. 2003. "The Delacroix Isleños and the Trappers' War in St. Bernard Parish." *Louisiana History: The Journal of the Louisiana History Association*. Vol. 44 (4): 411-441.

Hyland, William de Marigny. 2012. *Tour of Historic Saint Bernard Parish*. St. Bernard, Louisiana: Los Isleños Museum and Cultural Center.

Kniffen, Fred B., Hiram F. Gregory, and George A. Stokes. 1987. *The Historic Indian Tribes of Louisiana: From 1542 to the Present*. Baton Rouge: Louisiana State University Press.

Jackson, Raymond "Moose." 2009. *The Loup Garou: A Lunar Cycle*. New Orleans: Lavender Ink.

Jolivétte, Andrew. 2007. *Louisiana Creoles: Cultural Recovery and Mixed-Race Native American Identity*. Lanham, Maryland: Lexington Books.

Morrow, Susan Brind. "Trembling Prairie" in *Home Ground: A Guide to the American Landscape*. Edited by Barry Lopez and Debra Gwartney. San Antonio: Trinity University Press: 370.

Robertson, Morgan. "Swamp Lands Acts" in *Encyclopedia of Environment and Society*. Edited by Paul Robbins. Thousand Oaks: Sage Publications.

Swanton, John Reed. 1946. *The Indians of the Southeastern United States*. Washington D.C.: U.S. Government Printing Office.

Usner, Daniel. 2018. *American Indians in Early New Orleans: From Calumet to Raquette*. Baton Rouge: Louisiana State University Press.

———. 1992. *Indians, Settlers, and Slaves in a Frontier Exchange Economy: The Lower Mississippi Valley before 1783*. Chapel Hill: University of North Carolina Press.

Verdin, Monique. 2013. "Southward into the Vanishing Lands" in *Unfathomable City: A New Orleans Atlas*. Edited by Rebecca Solnit and Rebecca Snedeker. Berkeley: University of California Press.

Wells, Ken. "Matine's Dilemna" in *The Good Pirates of the Forgotten Bayous: Fighting to Save a Way of Life in the Wake of Katrina*. New Haven: Yale University Press: 56-68.

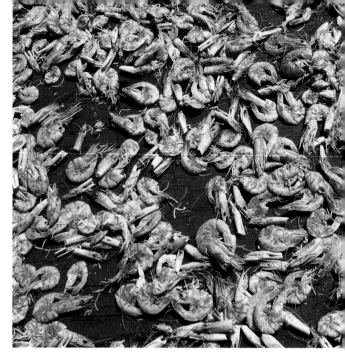

Dried Shrimp | 2007 | **Bayou Pointe-aux-Chenes**